CULTIVATE
THE PROCESS OF LIVING FROM YOUR HEART

cultivate
cul·ti·vate \ˈkəl-tə-ˌvāt\

: to prepare and use for the raising of crops
: to loosen or break up the soil
: to foster the growth of
: to improve by labor, care, or study
: further, encourage
: to seek the society of
: make friends with

IN THESE PAGES, YOU WILL FIND STORIES AND TEACHINGS THAT CONNECT TO OUR COMMUNITY'S HONEST JOURNEY WITH GOD. OUR DESIRE IS THAT YOU WOULD ENGAGE EACH WRITING WITH YOUR WHOLE HEART AND DO THE WORK IT REQUIRES TO CULTIVATE A **THRIVING RELATIONSHIP** WITH THE FATHER, SON AND HOLY SPIRIT. MANY OF THESE ARTICLES END WITH A PROMPT TO JOURNAL THE VOICE OF THE LORD. JESUS SAYS IN JOHN 10:27, **"MY SHEEP HEAR MY VOICE,** AND I KNOW THEM, AND THEY FOLLOW ME." AS A CHILD OF GOD, YOU HAVE ACCESS TO HIS VOICE, YOU CAN HEAR HIM, AND IT IS IMPORTANT THAT YOU RECORD, SAVOR AND DECLARE HIS THOUGHTS OVER YOUR LIFE. WHEN YOU JOURNAL HIS THOUGHTS, YOU WILL REMEMBER HOW DEEPLY HE LOVES YOU AND WHO YOU TRULY ARE. WE ENCOURAGE YOU TO **CENTER YOUR HEART** IN THIS SIMPLE TRUTH: GOD IS A LOVING FATHER, READY AND EAGER TO SPEAK TO YOU.

RECIPES and PROMPTS

01

25	The Quilt
52	Learning To Hear
55	Are You Enjoying God?
58	A Simple Question
72	Grains Of Sand
75	Finding Home
76	Listen Again
83	The Bench
84	Unlocking Grief
93	Big Hands, Tiny Wings
102	My Everyday Ocean
108	Eyes To See
110	Five Minute Prompts
113	Crops

RECIPES to PRACTICE REPENTANCE

02

31	The Mustard Seed And The Storm
35	We Become Free
47	The Pain Of A Fruitless Garden
49	Your Thoughts Define Me
78	Trusting His Nature
81	Discovering God's Goodness
94	The Patient Teacher
99	Filters

CREATIVE WRITINGS and STORIES

03

- 12   Cageless Birds
- 33   A Dare
- 40   Our Home Is Built With Yellow
- 45   Driftwood
- 50   The Well
- 56   The Wind And The Rain
- 65   Savor
- 73   Opening Up
- 85   The Birch
- 87   Does The Ocean Sleep Alone?
- 89   Feature on Ken Helser
- 103   The Language Of Hands
- 105   The In Between
- 112   Song Of The Morning

TOOLS and TEACHINGS

04

- 10   Keys For Cultivating Relationship
- 15   The Head To Heart Journey
- 22   Common Barriers
- 27   The Meeting Place
- 37   How Do I Partner With God?
- 42   He Didn't Hide Himself
- 61   Breath Prayer
- 62   The Art Of Being Answered
- 96   Your Heart Is A Garden
- 106   The Power Of Scripture

*ON THE SHORES OF MY SOUL,
I GIVE YOU PERMISSION.*

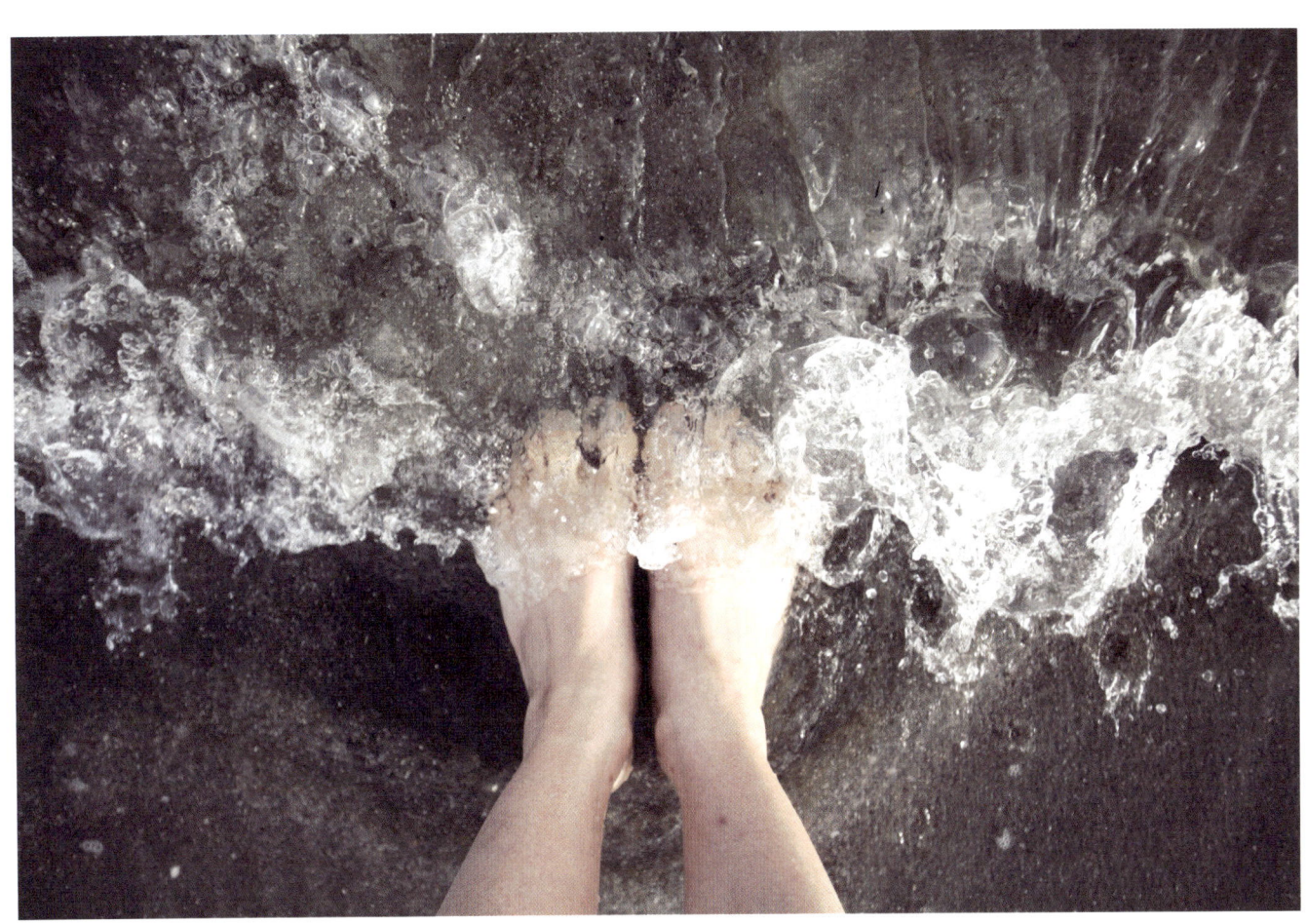

WHAT IS / CULTI- VATE?

a note from the editor

Cultivate is a devotional series our community lovingly put together to help you connect with God in your daily life. We chose the name *Cultivate* because we love what it means. One of the definitions is "to foster the growth of,"[2] and we believe that every human heart is worth the reward of growth. Growth fills our hearts with courage and faith. When we see it in our lives, we remember that Jesus is fighting for us, hope is real and that change is possible.

The metaphor of our hearts being like a garden is one we come back to often. We believe that growth and maturity in our faith requires both our willingness to do the work and the presence of God to bless that work and make things grow. We do the work of planting, tilling, pruning—and God does the work of sending the sun and the rain. We are entirely dependent on Him, and as we commit to our part, He makes things grow.

We understand that "doing the work" is a concept that's simple enough in theory, but is much more difficult to put into practice. It can be tough to know where to start. What does "the work" actually mean, and what does it really look like to take care of your heart? The purpose of *Cultivate* is to help define the work by giving you a starting place. Our intention is to empower you to initiate this work with the Lord and to offer starting points for connection with Him. These books have been intentionally written and designed to help you connect with your own heart and with God. If your heart is a garden, then these books are designed to give you tools that help you plant, uproot, harvest and prune so that you may thrive. In this series you'll find stories from our personal experiences, testimonies, poetry, artwork and questions to ask the Lord. Our hope is that each page will serve as a tool to help you, empower you, inspire you and lead you to relief and connection in your walk with Jesus.

The gift of gardening is that it yields a reward that ultimately nourishes you and the ones you care about. Good fruit and vegetables serve to fill us, satisfy our needs and bring delight. Our prayer is that, as you commit to taking care of your heart, you feel the reward of your life bearing good fruit. You are called to live a fruitful life! Throughout this book, you'll see the term "Recipe". This is the term we've chosen for our writings that offer both a testimony and a practical application, such as a journaling prompt or a directive to take action. We chose the word "recipe" because these writings are intended to help you harvest the fruit from your

life and turn it into something that you can feast on. For example: "A Recipe for Opening Up" might end with a prompt that instructs you to practice vulnerability, so that your need for connection with others may be satisfied. We charge you to not just read these recipes but to complete the prompts—this is the difference between just looking at the fruit in your garden and actually eating it. We bless you to not only produce good fruit, but enjoy it!

by MELISSA HELSER

KEYS for CULTIVATING a RELATIONSHIP

In the following pages, you will be introduced to foundational keys to cultivating a relationship with the Trinity. These are the foundations upon which all of our *Cultivate* books are written, and are the heartbeat of this series. As you read these keys, may you find your heart filled with hope and inspiration to continue cultivating a deep and lasting friendship with the Father, Son and Holy Spirit.

01. Emotions & Vulnerability

"He became Human! He humbled himself and became vulnerable, choosing to be revealed as a man and was obedient. He was a perfect example, even in his death—a criminal's death by crucifixion!" (Philippians 2:7-8, TPT). Emotions are the language of the heart. God, as an emotional being Himself, gave emotions to us as indicators to help us understand how we are being affected by life and what we need. They were not meant to be blindly followed, but instead, they were designed to be a meeting place of conversation with the Holy Spirit. Emotions help us acknowledge and talk about what's really going on so that we can live life fully awake. We don't have to fear our emotions when they are submitted to Jesus.

It is impossible to understand our emotions without practicing vulnerability with ourselves. Stopping and acknowledging our feelings can be an incredibly brave and valuable action. Inviting the Holy Spirit into this process is an essential part of a healthy relationship with God and one of our greatest privileges as sons and daughters. When we practice putting our heart language to words by being honest, asking for help, confessing, repenting and rejoicing to God, we practice vulnerability. We cannot thrive in our relationship with God without vulnerability.

02. Asking Good Questions

"Show me your ways, Lord, teach me your paths. Guide me in your truth and teach me, for you are God my Savior, and my hope is in you all day long" (Psalm 25:4-5, NIV). We are shaped by the questions we ask God. Questions open our hearts to hear His response and give Him the opportunity to bring truth and clarity. If we do not ask God about the things that matter most, as well as the little things that may seem to not matter at all, we will have a stunted, compartmentalized relationship with Him. God is full of vision for our lives and fully present in every moment. Learning how to go to Him for wisdom, as opposed to trying to prove we already know, is a mark of maturity and love. It is our honor, not our shame, to need His affirmation, guidance and clarity.

03. The Voice of the Lord

"My sheep hear my voice, and I know them, and they follow me" (John 10:27, ESV). We are shaped by the voices we listen to, and if we do not know how to hear the Lord's voice, we will become like the lesser voices we listen to. We must learn how to lean in, listen and respond as He speaks to us through Scripture, through journaling His voice and through the gift of our imaginations. We need His voice to bring our whole selves into alignment with truth. Without the voice of the Lord—His daily interaction with us—our relationship with Him can feel one-sided and distant. God longs for us to know His voice and to let Him encourage and correct us as He leads us into truth.

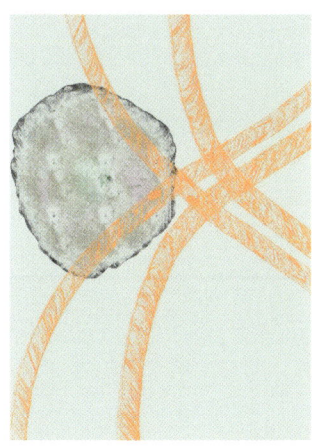

04. Receiving from Beauty

"One thing I ask from the Lord, this only do I seek: that I may dwell in the house of the Lord all the days of my life, to gaze on the beauty of the Lord and to seek him in his temple" (Psalm 27:4, NIV). In everything, God has a voice. He loves to speak to us and move us through beauty. As we learn to quiet our hearts and minds, to shed our judgments and pride, we begin to see Him everywhere and grow an ability to receive Him in anything. The beauty of the Lord is all around us, inviting us to be inspired as we seek Him. As we approach life with curiosity and begin to wonder, *How could the Lord be speaking to me through this?* We find that He is always near.

05. Repentance

"God's kindness is intended to lead you to repentance" (Romans 2:4, NIV). Repentance is an incredible gift. It goes far beyond behavioral management and brings us into deep transformation. Repentance is when we stop hiding. It is the moment we turn back home to encounter a Father running to meet us with redemption. This is the place we really get honest with God and exchange the lies we have believed for God's truth about us. When we practice repentance, we receive God's forgiveness and let it restore our connection to Him, to ourselves and to others. God longs for us to do the beautiful work of repentance so He can give us all that He has in His heart for us.

with the TRINITY

by the CULTIVATE TEAM
art by MORGAN CAMPBELL and JUSTINA STEVENS

CAGELESS BIRDS

Standing on the shore of decision
looking into the face of adventure,
desire to abandon all I know.
What pushes me is rooted
somewhere between misunderstanding
and knowing.
Knowing what I want to understand
is not within my reach.
So I ponder my escape
not knowing what lies ahead.

Adventure in theory is full of excitement
and bleeds with passion for life.
But adventure in reality
is full of breathless moments,
silent nights
and wounds that leave scars
of memory on a heart.
Can I go the distance?
Can I give all of my mind to get what the
Messenger is saying?

by MELISSA HELSER
photograph by CADENCE HELSER

Can I surrender my unknowing?
Will I survive the humility of ignorance
to obtain a treasure earthly gold cannot buy?
Will I ask the question of honesty
even if the answer convicts my soul
and sends me to the land of repentance?

All of these thoughts flood my mind
as I stand on the shore of choosing
and in the distance of my wondering,
I see with clear eyes
A flock of wild, beautiful birds
swooping clearly in my direction
as if they see me and are coming for me.
And how strange it is that their eyes
are full of clarity
and the melody of their flapping wings—
they sing out,
We are coming for you.

the HEAD *to* HEART JOURNEY

by JONATHAN DAVID HELSER / art by JUSTINA STEVENS

I was twenty years old the first time I heard the phrase "Head to Heart Journey" from an old cowboy named Mickey Evans. It was in the swamps of Florida, at an old pole barn behind Mickey's house where he hosted a small Sunday school. Mickey is a hero in the Kingdom. He gave his life to build a rehabilitation center for men to be set free from addiction. I will never forget looking him in the eyes for the first time. He's one of those people whose face would glow from his friendship with Jesus. His eyes were like oceans of love. When Mickey would talk about Jesus, he would cry every time.

Mickey said, "Today for Sunday school, I want to ask you a question: Where does Jesus live?" Of course, we were all good Christians, we knew Jesus lives in our hearts. Mickey said, "Yes, and now I want to take you guys on an 18 Inch Journey. That's the distance from your head to your heart." He said, "There's a set of steps and I want you to imagine them. The steps begin in your head and they lead down to this beautiful room that's in your heart. In this room are two chairs: in one of the chairs, Jesus is sitting. And beside Him there's an empty chair, and He's waiting for you to come sit with Him. To be with Him. To be known by Him and to pour out your heart to Him."

And so Mickey prayed and led us through a prompt, "Let's take that journey. Now I want you to open your journals and write to Jesus, as He's sitting in that chair, your most honest prayer. Just pour your heart out to Him. What you're feeling, what you're thinking." So we all began to write. Then Mickey said, "When you finish the prayer, I want you to skip a line and just simply lean in. You're there with Jesus and I want you to journal what Jesus thinks and feels about you." It was a life-changing moment. Little did I know, Mickey was helping me dig a well that I would drink from for the rest of my life. Learning how to be honest and vulnerable before God, then stepping back and letting God speak His thoughts back over me.

To me, that's the essence of what the Head to Heart Journey is. It's learning to make this journey into our hearts and really listen. It's a place of vulnerability before God. A place of abundant life as we move beyond facts we know about Him in our heads and into this place of intimate knowledge of who God is and who He made us to be. Twenty years later, this Head to Heart Journey is a value system that Melissa and I are still walking out. It's much more than a volume of *Cultivate*. It is a value we have chosen to live by, and it's a reality in the Kingdom.

I grew up in church and one of the things I heard a lot was, "Don't trust your feelings or emotions. You have to trust in the Lord." And part of that is true, but part of that is really misleading. For years, the belief that I couldn't trust my emotions led me to a place of denying what was going on in my heart. I was hiding my true emotions from God, and really, hiding my emotions from myself. I wasn't listening to my heart.

Our emotions are the language that our hearts speak. They are a part of our lives that need to be valued and respected. I believe that they are a gift from God that help us understand what is going on inside of us. We can actually begin to listen to these emotions and let them lead us to Jesus. We don't blindly follow them, which was the caution we were hearing in church: *Don't be led by your emotions.* But we are meant to listen to them, and let them become a meeting place with God. It's when we acknowledge our emotions that we can submit them to the Lord, and then trust Him to lead us. And as we start this journey, it begins to guide us into wholeness and integration.

There's a beautiful quote from Tremper Longman and Dan Allender in *The Cry of the Soul* that really sums up what I'm saying about emotions and how we are connected to our hearts. It says:

"Ignoring our emotions is turning our back on reality. Listening to our emotions ushers us into reality. And reality is where we meet God… Emotions are the language of the soul. They are the cry that gives the heart a voice… However, we often turn a deaf ear—through emotional denial, distortion, or disengagement. We strain out anything disturbing in order to gain tenuous control of our inner world. We are frightened and ashamed of what leaks into our consciousness. In neglecting our intense emotions, we are false to ourselves and lose a wonderful opportunity to know God. We forget that change comes through brutal honesty and vulnerability before God.",[3]

I love the last line of this quote. "We forget that change comes through brutal honesty and vulnerability before God." It sounds scary, but I promise it is worth it. Emotions have a way of revealing our needs, our deep-seated beliefs and our passions. When we give space to our emotions, expressing what's inside of us, they become pathways into deeper intimacy with the Father, and they allow Him to meet us in the parts of our souls where we need Him most. This intimacy with God in every part of our lives, in all the different spaces of our hearts, is really where abundant life begins.

One of my heroes in Scripture is David. He lived in a place of brutal honesty and vulnerability before God, and he is given this name at the end of his life for all of history: a man after God's own heart. David was a man full of wild emotion. From the highest high to the lowest low, we see David live this vulnerable life before God, and we're still getting to read the songs he wrote where he poured out his honest emotions. They became Scripture—something we're going to read forever. That's how much God loves our emotions. I don't know what it is inside of me that wants to hide my emotions from God. I did this for years. Maybe I thought it would make Him angry. But I've learned that full life—abundant life—comes when I begin to get in touch with my heart and submit my emotions to God.

I love the book of Psalms and how it helps me get in touch with my emotions. I was recently reading back through them, and these were just a few of the emotions that I found: loneliness,

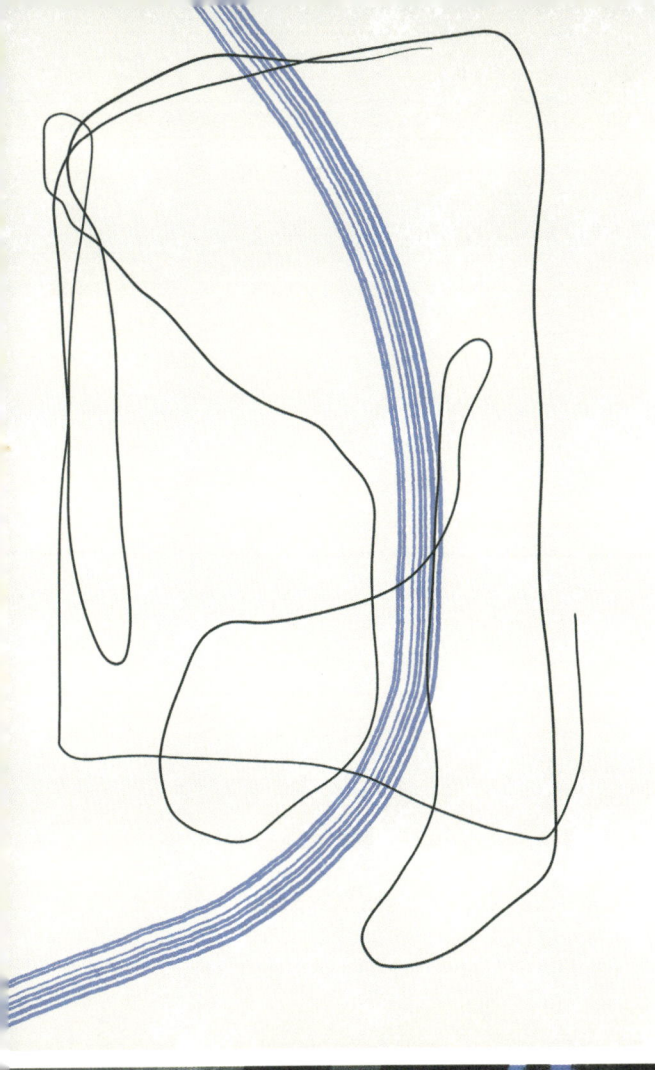

Our emotions are the language that our hearts speak. They are a part of our lives that need to be valued and respected. I believe that they are a gift from God that help us understand what is going on inside of us.

sorrow, regret, shame, discouragement, joy, gladness, delight, fear, anger, peace, grief, hope, gratitude, zeal, heaviness, confidence. You can find almost every human emotion somewhere in the book of Psalms because David literally lived in this place of naked trust before God. Remember when he nearly strips off all of his clothes to dance before the ark and before God? I think in that moment, when he was dancing before the ark, he was dancing his way back into Eden. He was returning to what Adam and Eve had left behind—walking hand in hand with the Father with nothing left between his heart and the Father's heart. He lived in that place of honesty.

If you think about this human compulsion to hide from God, it started in Eden when we believed the first lie. If you remember, Adam and Eve took a bite of the suspicion that God wasn't good when the serpent said, "Did God really say…?" And the first thing they did was feel shame and hide themselves from God. The good news is the Father is walking through your garden right now. He's walking through your heart saying, "Where are you?" St. Augustine sums it up in a really beautiful way, "How can you draw close to God when you're far from your own self?"[4] What I've learned is that as I make that Head to Heart Journey—by listening to what is happening in my heart and opening myself up to the voice of the Father—then I am actually drawing close to Him.

I really want you to feel the weight and value of the reality that your emotions are the voice of your heart. To take this a little deeper, let's go from David to Jesus. Jesus was a man full of emotion. We see Him in wild joy feasting at a wedding, and then in deep sorrow as He weeps over Jerusalem. We see Him in pain in the Garden of Gethsemane. We see Him at peace when He's sleeping through the storm. We see anger burst out of Him at the religious spirit as He's flipping tables over. We see Him at His friend's funeral, weeping before the tomb and then roaring resurrection, calling Lazarus out of the grave. We see Him surprised at the faith of a Roman centurion. We see so many emotions in Jesus, and He said, "If you've seen me, you've seen the Father" (John 14:9, CEV). That means God is emotional. You're emotional. You're just like your Father.

Another quote that's really helped me in my journey of learning to value my heart and listen to my emotions comes from Chip Dodd in his book, *The Voice of the Heart*. He says,

"When you begin to recognize and listen to your heart again, it will recognize you and guide you to the place where you can start to live life in openness. This openness will take you to fuller, richer living through relationship. To acknowledge that truth is to become vulnerable to your heart. Vulnerability exposes neediness, and neediness can lead us to seeking and knowing others and God. Simply put, if we do these three things—feel our feelings, tell the truth, and give it to God—full life will follow. The process of life, God created."[5]

Connecting with God in our emotions is not intuitive for most of us, but it is possible. If practiced, this Head to Heart Journey will forge a path of connection between you and the Father. You are worth the process of journeying from your head to your heart and back again to enter into vulnerability and full life with God.

Prompt: Today, I want to help you get started in taking this journey from your head to your heart. On the next page is a tool that includes three steps that are actually quite easy, but they will require vulnerability and they will require honesty.

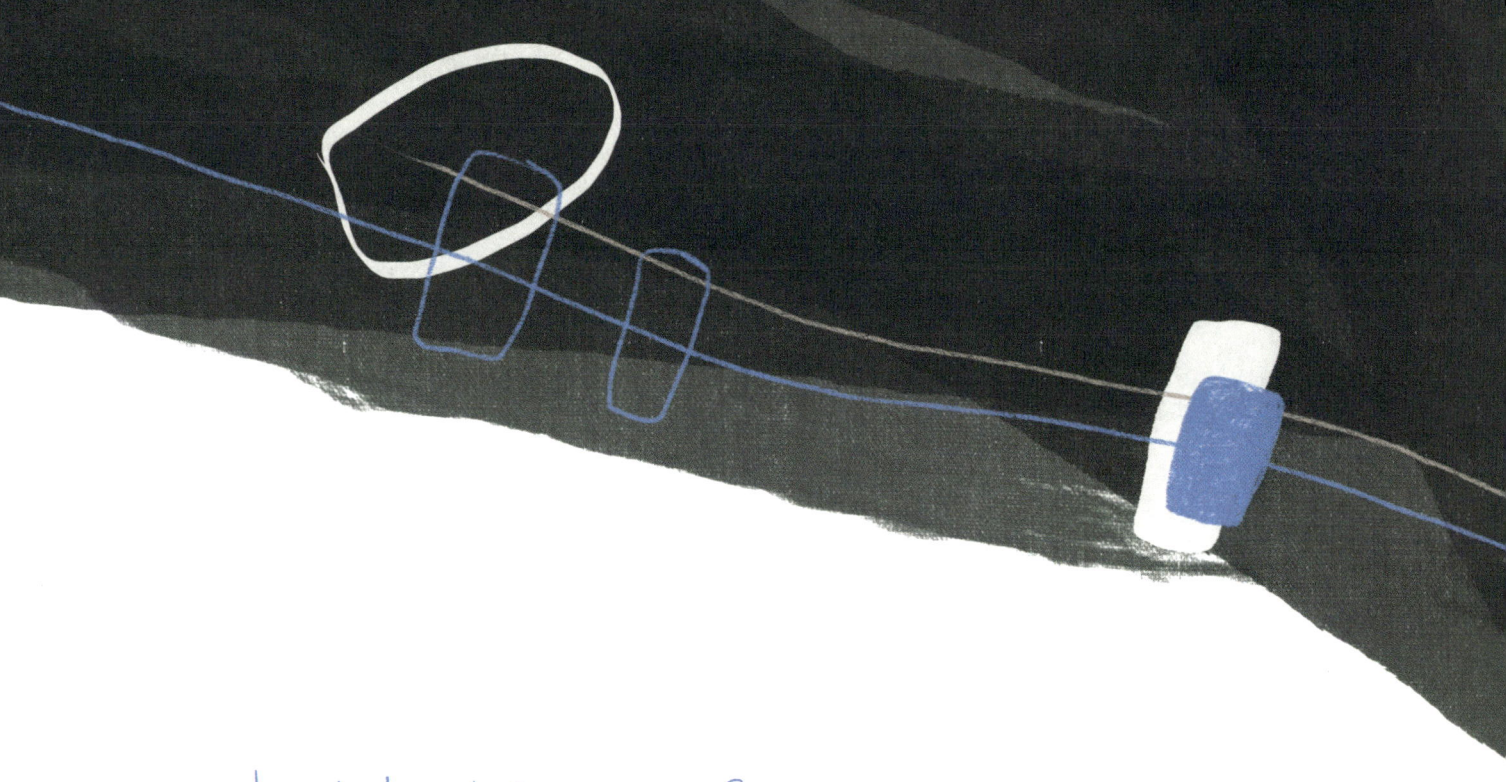

1. Identify your feelings

Slow down and make the journey into your heart. Take a deep breath. Ask yourself: "What am I feeling right now?" Then write down three to five emotions.

2. Be Honest

Write an honest prayer to God and use all of the feelings that you named in Step One. While you are writing the prayer, I encourage you to pull up our Cageless Birds album titled *Generosity*, and listen to the song titled: The Head to Heart Journey. Let it play in the background and inspire you to make the journey from your head to your heart.

3. Allow God to Respond and help

First, read your honest prayer you've just written out loud to the Lord. Then, let the song play again. Give God space to respond to this question: "God, what are your thoughts and feelings about me right now?" By faith, write what you hear and feel the Lord speaking to your heart. Once you're finished, read God's words over yourself out loud. The Head to Heart Journey is also the journey back from your heart to your head and your mouth. You will begin to speak and think differently as your core beliefs begin to change. Transformation happens from the inside out.

Well done! This is a practice that you can come back to any time. I encourage you to listen to your heart and learn to live in radical trust with God like David. You are worth processing your emotions with God.

BASKETS
drawing by JUSTINA STEVENS

BUT JESUS SAID, "THERE IS NO NEED TO DISMISS THEM. YOU GIVE THEM SUPPER."

"ALL WE HAVE ARE FIVE LOAVES OF BREAD AND TWO FISH," THEY SAID.

JESUS SAID, "BRING THEM HERE."

THEN HE HAD THE PEOPLE SIT ON THE GRASS. HE TOOK THE FIVE LOAVES AND TWO FISH, LIFTED HIS FACE TO HEAVEN IN PRAYER, BLESSED, BROKE, AND GAVE THE BREAD TO THE DISCIPLES. THE DISCIPLES THEN GAVE THE FOOD TO THE CONGREGATION. THEY ALL ATE THEIR FILL. THEY GATHERED TWELVE BASKETS OF LEFTOVERS. ABOUT FIVE THOUSAND WERE FED.

MATTHEW 14:16-21, MSG

COMMON BARRIERS WHEN JOURNALING the VOICE of the LORD

by JOEL CASE

"...People do not live by bread alone, but by every word that comes from the mouth of God" (Matthew 4:4, NLT).

We are made to hear God's voice and thrive in relationship with Him. This is an integral part of our design and inheritance as human beings. What could be more valuable than knowing the personal voice of the Father, Son and Holy Spirit? And now, through Jesus, we have been granted free access to hear what God is saying to us every day!

One way I engage the voice of the Lord is through journaling. I sit down, get quiet and write the flow of thoughts and sentences that I hear God speaking to me. It's a conversation I engage on purpose, leaning in to listen and receive. In my life, hearing His voice in a consistent way, pen to paper, has been a simple yet profound pathway to God's heart. His voice often resets and makes sense of what's going on inside me. I show up cloudy and come out clear; heavy and He lifts my head. I've often been carried by just one sentence through my day that kept me aware of His love and presence.

I want to help make this practice accessible to you. As you start journaling the voice of the Lord, you're going to notice that there are real barriers that come against your connection with God. We all hit walls on this journey and need help to stand up in our faith. I'm going to address the five most common barriers to journaling God's voice that we, as a community, have discovered along the way.

BARRIER I
"That was just me thinking those things, not God speaking..."

TRUTH
"...we have the mind of Christ" (I Corinthians 2:16, NIV).

Most of the time you will hear God's voice through your thoughts because God lives inside of you. Thoughts are one way you "hear." This should be taken as a sign of God's closeness to you, not of distance or immaturity. One thing to note here is that God doesn't only speak through words and sentences. He also may speak through an image or moving picture in your mind. Or He may communicate through a feeling, where you can sense His intentions with your heart. These are just a few ways He speaks. Sometimes in the moment of writing these thoughts, pictures or impressions down, I'll have doubts of whether what I am hearing is God or just me. Maybe I was having an off day, maybe my mind or emotions felt foggy. But so often, if I read back over it, I am surprised by the clarity and accuracy of what I journaled. I am also surprised by the tone; God always speaks with such kindness and power. I've learned over the years that His tone is very different from the tone I use with myself. You don't always have to "feel it" when you write. When doubt comes, go back and reread His words.

BARRIER II

"Presuming to hear and write God's voice down is dangerous because it is subjective, diminishes the authority of the Bible and ultimately could lead us astray. It's too risky, and we have the Bible anyways. Let's stay safe."

TRUTH

"My sheep hear my voice, and I know them, and they follow me" (John 10:27, ESV).

The clearest and most direct answer to this barrier is that Jesus neither lived this way, nor taught His followers to. He grew up knowing and valuing the Scriptures and also personally heard what the Father was saying (see John 12:49). So following Jesus means learning Scripture *and* leaning in to hear the Father. We can be confident that what God speaks will always resonate with what He spoke in the pages of the Bible. Scripture is full of the voice of God and gives us a level ground to practice on. But it's both, not one or the other. Jesus said, "You search the Scriptures because you think that in them you have eternal life; and it is they that bear witness about me, yet you refuse to come to me that you may have life" (John 5:39-40, ESV). The Bible reveals Jesus so that we can come into personal relationship with Him.

BARRIER III

"I should hear perfect the first time, every word must be God's voice dictated onto the page."

TRUTH

"...[Enoch] was commended as having pleased God. And without faith it is impossible to please him, for whoever would draw near to God must believe that he exists and that he rewards those who seek him" (Hebrews 11:5-6, ESV).

We have to take the pressure off! God is a good Father who is moved by our efforts to love and seek Him. He gave His only Son to have us back in this relationship. He is not stingy, legalistic or cruel. When we move toward God it moves His heart. As with anything, hearing God's voice takes practice. We will grow in hearing God more clearly as we mature and our trust deepens. But unhealthy pressure will hinder our ability to show up and engage in peace and trust. Here is a prayer if you feel stuck in this barrier: "God, you invited me to learn how to hear your voice, and you are not pressuring me to do it perfectly. I take off that unrealistic expectation, and lean into the belief that you are pleased by my attempts to get to know you."

BARRIER IV

"This is just wishful thinking, it's too good to be true."

TRUTH

"Now to him who is able to do far more abundantly than all that we ask or think, according to the power at work within us, to him be glory..." (Ephesians 3:20-21, ESV).

When we're brave enough to get honest and look at what is underneath the mindset of, *It's too good to be true*, we'll almost always find places where we feel shame and unworthiness. It's hard to trust in the Lord's generous and encouraging voice when we feel unworthy of it, so it's easier to write it off as just "wishful thinking." And when we have traded our confidence and faith for unhealthy shame, it becomes way harder to hear God! Think of this like a garden hose. God is the source, open and flowing with water, and a crimp in the hose (a crimp of shame, unworthiness, distrust) keeps that water from reaching us. It's not on God's end, He is not withholding any good thing from us (see Romans 8:32, James 1:17, I Timothy 4:4, Matthew 7:11). When this barrier comes up, we can take a moment to ask God to help us undo the crimp; we can choose to open up to being more loved than we feel we are. Because this shame issue won't be resolved without love. We can choose trust and confidence again. He desires to uproot our unbelief through the power of His voice!

THE PRESSURE IS OFF & THE INVITATION TO PRACTICE & LEARN IS ON!

BARRIER V

"I am afraid to journal God's voice. What if God punishes or condemns me?"

TRUTH

"There is therefore now no condemnation for those who are in Christ Jesus" (Romans 8:1, ESV).

Hearing God's voice has as much to do with receiving His tone as it does the actual words. Think about how important this is in communication with another person. It's one reason texting can be so hard! I see the words they wrote…but what is their tone? The Holy Spirit conveys the tone of God to our hearts (see Romans 5:5). And since what He says to you won't go against Scripture, there will never be any condemnation in His voice. It is important to remember that we need God's voice to encourage as well as correct us. God's correction is a good gift. We need to learn His tone in moments when we have messed up. Leaning into God's voice when we have sinned or made a mistake is one of the most powerful things we can do. In my journey, as I press past my fears and practice hearing His voice, I've slowly discovered just how kind, gracious and compassionate He really is.

Prompt: Grab a journal and something to write with. Flip to a clean page and write down this question: "God, what's one thing you want to help me with this week?" Close your eyes and take a deep breath. Let your faith rise. Remember, God cares enough to respond. When you start to sense something, put your pen to paper and begin to write what comes into your mind! Let the Lord's thoughts flow, practicing moving through any of the barriers you read about, and just try. You might hear a few sentences, you might hear pages. Typically, you'll hit a point where you feel a rest come, a pause. When you feel this, breathe out a, "Thank you, Lord." Then reread what He said. Let it affect you! Underline one sentence of what He said and practice remembering it throughout the day. Let it connect you to the God who loves to speak to His children.

Here's my example: "Joel, my beloved, I am so glad you asked. I want to help you turn your motivation from fear to an active belief in my goodness. A courageous belief! A confident belief founded on belonging. I want to challenge the places in you that still argue their position that you are not worthy. That narrative is still attached in your soul, and I am set on separating it from you. When your sense of belonging is accused and taken from you, and you find yourself reaching for the fuel of fear to help drive you to fix it, turn toward me instead. Ask for my help, and I will restore you. I will give back what has been taken. Don't try to fight the enemy on your own, driving around in the fear of rejection. You are not on your own. Not with me, not with my family around you. Come to me when you feel afraid. That is the courage and resilience I am talking about. Maintain your belonging above appeasing the lies. Don't give it up to anything or anyone! You are bold and brave and I am growing you as a champion. Don't lose heart. I love you and am so proud of you and your growth!"

THE QUILT

RECIPE FOR RECEIVING GOD'S PRESENCE

"He alone is my safe place; his wraparound presence always protects me. For he is my champion defender; there's no risk of failure with God. So why would I let worry paralyze me, even when troubles multiply around me?" Psalm 62:2, TPT

I have often been envious of people who have family quilts; handcrafted treasures passed down from generation to generation. These bearers of stories and comfort are possessions to be valued. They lie draped over the sides of beds, beckoning to be touched and felt. They find a way to unfold their affectionate arms around the shoulders of small, drowsy children around the crackling fireplace. They're brought outside to grassy summer picnics. They're swiftly unfurled when toes feel the icy bite on winter evenings.

I had always wanted this kind of cherished friend to preserve memories and secrets for me, the royal heir. Sadly, my parents never had a fondness for blankets. Perhaps they never had a need for these swollen covers in the stifling, equator-centered cities they lived in for so long. It wasn't until I was a young adult that I discovered an appreciation for these soft, weighty shelters—useful when feeling sick, playful, sneaky or sleepy.

When I received my first quilt as a gift from a dear friend a couple of years ago, I wept with happiness. It was the real thing—not skimpy, deflated or fleece. It reached out to hug me with its full body and peaceful colors. Its flowering grandness cooed to my heart, "You are warm and safe." It has reminded me many a night, as I have drifted off to Dreamland, that I am loved; a favorite and secure babe in the embrace of Strength and Gentleness.

The Lord is my Quilt and my Great Comforter. I didn't know or appreciate His tender warmth and substantial shelter for so long in my life. I wish I had recognized His safety sooner, so I could have felt the peace and steady breathing in my spirit. So I could have listened to His whispered secrets. So I could have fallen asleep in His beauty and rested my heart. But His grace meets me yet again, and I am a child once more. I have found the Ultimate Playmate, the Almighty Healer and the Divine Peace-bringer. The Lord is my Quilt and my Great Comforter.

Prompt: Close your eyes and take a deep breath. Imagine God's presence wrapping around you like a blanket today. Let the simplicity of engaging your imagination with God be enough today.

by ERIN GRAVITT

PRESSURE IS REAL.

Throughout my life I have felt a tremendous pressure to be and act a certain way. There are so many unspoken expectations that hang over our hearts and minds. In my twenties as I wrestled deeply with an auto-immune disease, got married, had children and began leading a ministry, I started feeling suffocated by the pressure. Some days I could barely get out of bed because of the physical pain, other days the exhaustion took an overwhelming toll, but still I pushed myself to be and do what I really had no capacity for. "Do it for the Glory of God," I would hear in my mind. People would ask how I was and I would smile and say, "I am okay, and God is so good." I couldn't come face-to-face with the reality that I was sinking into a very dark and lonely place. When I would practice the smallest amount of honesty, I would often hear, "The Lord is gonna use this season for His glory."

Use…I don't want to be used. I want to be loved and cared for.

When I look back to over twenty years ago, I see a very frustrated, tired and hurting Melissa. I see a Melissa that was craving permission to be in pain without being given quick, religious answers to things that actually weren't that simple. In one of my most frustrating moments I heard the Lord say to me, "Melissa if you will give me back my humanity, I will give you back yours." This statement felt confusing, but I knew that God was inviting me into a season of understanding something I had no real concept of: His humanity.

We love to focus on the divinity of Jesus, the power and the reverence of God in our human form. But what about the reality of Philippians 2? "…though he was in the form of God, did not count equality with God a thing to be grasped, but emptied himself, by taking the form of a servant, being born in the likeness of men" (Philippians 2:6-7, ESV). God clothed Himself in limitation, relinquished Himself to capacity and yielded to being human.

The more I read and meditated on this truth, the more I felt met very deeply. As I dove into the actual truth of Jesus as a man and the full range of human limitation He felt, the more I exhaled all the pressure to be super-human. We can see Jesus in every stage: a baby, a child, an adult that gets hungry and tired. We see a man that feels deep sadness and overwhelming delight. We observe a Christ that is full of compassion for the broken, the outcast and then simultaneously willing to demonstrate and fully feel grief and sorrow. We read about Him going away to pray and be alone. He was a man who lingered in a place and said no when His friends asked Him to come and help. He was misunderstood and often accused, felt disappointment and longed for companionship.

He was a human and this is our Jesus. Not a distant and far away Savior, but a God who desires for us to feel seen and understood, so much so that He put on our flesh and bone and remains in that body for eternity. This was and is a wave of relief for me. Webster defines "relief" as a: "removal or lightening of something oppressive, painful, or distressing.". That definition is extremely accurate for me and probably for you, too. Can we embrace the relief that comes from understanding that we do not have a high priest who cannot sympathize with our weaknesses? (see Hebrews 4:15) He sympathizes, understands and has compassion for us. He is not rushing and urging me to get over it, pull up my boot straps and push through. He is covering me in empathy and speaking kindly to my tired heart.

by MELISSA HELSER / *photography by* MORGAN CAMPBELL

Our humanity is a gift, not a hindrance, it is a meeting place between our heart and the heart of Jesus.

Whatever season you're in and whatever age you are, we all know what it is like to feel pressure coming at us from all sides. Whether it is from friends, parents, church culture or work, we all can relate to desiring a better way. Understanding the fullness of Jesus the human gives me a lot of permission, and permission is really important to understand as you give in to seasons of growth and maturing. If we are to be "like Christ" then we are to look at, imitate and be inspired by His life as a human. He gives us permission to be as He was. Our humanity is a gift, it is not a hindrance, but a meeting place between our hearts and the heart of Jesus. It is permission to be and learn and grow. Permission to not know yet. To give in to seasons of newness and seasons of looking back. To yield to the process of becoming.

The more I gave in to His life and let it transform so many of my patterns, the more confidence I had in my own process. I began to ask myself better questions. Ones like: *Melissa, do you have capacity for this? Is that voice a lie or truth? Is the Lord inviting you to do this or is this pressure-driven? Are you tired and need to rest? What is Jesus saying right now?* These might seem simple and obvious, but for me they weren't at all. I was so used to "pressing through for the sake of the Gospel," that I had zero understanding of limits. Embracing my limits has changed my life. It has given me more capacity for loving myself and loving people than I ever thought possible. It has released me from shame-driven doing and landed me in a confident, powerful Yes or No.

Jesus didn't always say yes. When Martha and Mary sent word to Him that their brother was sick and to please come… He lingered where He was. He waited until it felt like it was too late. When He finally came, the sisters met Him, each with their own pain and disappointment. They knew that Jesus could have healed Lazarus, but did they know He could raise the dead? They knew Jesus cared for their brother but did they know the Jesus who weeps? In John 11, we read about His interaction with Mary: "When Jesus saw her weeping, and the Jews who had come with her also weeping, he was deeply moved in his spirit and greatly troubled. And he said, "Where have you laid him?" They said to him, "Lord, come and see." Jesus wept. So the Jews said, "See how he loved him!" (John 11:33-36, ESV).

This was before the resurrection, before the miracle! A stunning demonstration of humanness that moved the people to say, "See how he loved him!" I love this passage of Scripture so much because we see Jesus offering us human emotion and compassion before He does the supernatural. He meets us fully where we are and solidifies His love for us, then He performs miracles. Isn't this as great a miracle…receiving the affection and love of God and knowing that He deeply cares for our hurting hearts?

My charge to you is this: embrace your humanity not as a hindrance, but as a meeting place. Begin to ask Jesus to give you an understanding of His humanity so that you can receive your own. I challenge you to stop shaming yourself into transformation, but loving yourself into change, asking different questions and letting the Lord meet you in your limits as He strengthens you for your life. Embracing the humanity of Jesus has given me so much permission to grow and receive the pruning that maturity requires. It has released me from the pressure to perform for God and has nurtured a true and honest friendship with the person of Jesus. It has given me the confidence to ask God for sustained energy and strength when I need it, which is entirely different than living in denial to my limitations. This is the gift we have been given: a Savior that took on our human limits to show us the way. May you be inspired by His love to meet you where you are and feel the permission to receive your limits and grow in true friendship.

PRAYER AND PROMPT

Close your eyes. Take a deep breath. Pray this prayer: "Lord I am here. Jesus, thank you for loving me so deeply that you took on flesh and bone. I acknowledge and honor the generosity of your heart to meet me where I am. Thank you for walking this earth as a man, who experienced the full range of joy and sorrow, thriving and suffering. I receive the truth that you are not far away but close to me, and in this truth I ask you to show me where you are. Show me the places in my life that I have placed you far away from my everyday humanity. I reach for the meeting place of our shared human experience. I desire to see you as you are and let your humanity give me permission to be fully me. I give you back your humanity and receive the gift of mine. I look to you as my Savior, my Shepherd and my Friend. You are here with me. Give me the courage to receive you and be honest with where I am."

Ask yourself these questions: Where am I trying to prove myself to the Lord? Where are the places I am performing for Him instead of asking for help and acknowledging my limits?

Ask the Lord this question and journal His response: Where are you inviting me to be more honest with the frailty of my humanity so that I can receive your supernatural strength?

THE MUSTARD SEED & THE STORM

RECIPE FOR REPENTANCE
writing and drawing by JUSTINA STEVENS

"Again he said, 'what shall we say the kingdom of God is like, or what parable shall we use to describe it? It is like a mustard seed, which is the smallest of all seeds on earth. Yet when planted, it grows and becomes the largest of all garden plants, with such big branches that the birds can perch in its shade.' With many similar parables Jesus spoke the word to them, as much as they could understand. He did not say anything to them without using a parable. But when he was alone with his own disciples, he explained everything." Mark 4:30-34, NIV

The Bible doesn't tell us what Jesus said in secret to His disciples, but I like to imagine that He shared secrets with them and challenged them. I imagine Him looking into their eyes and speaking straight to their hearts. I imagine His disciples feeling empowered, like they could conquer the world. Yet later in the chapter, in verse 35, on that very same day Jesus said, "Let us cross over to the other side," and they got in a boat and set sail. Suddenly, a huge storm developed and the disciples lost control of the boat. The twelve, shaking in their boots and fearing for their lives, cried out to Jesus, "Don't you care if we die?" as He was sleeping below the deck.

Now, this is where many people would like to talk about the peace of Jesus that surpassed the anxiety of mankind to speak peace to a storm, which is true; but I'd like to point to a different avenue in this story. "Don't you care if we die?" The fear-stricken words that hit the air quickly. Jesus had just looked all of His disciples in the eyes hours before and told them the plain secrets of the Kingdom, and what surfaced in the storm was the disbelief in the disciples' hearts. I believe that in that meeting hours before, Jesus was charging the boys to believe, to trust, to receive an upgrade in their faith. Who knows? Perhaps He was preparing them for their faith to be tested. Was the panic the disciples experienced and the questioning of Jesus *failure*? I don't know. What I am sure of is this: the disciples could see exactly how immature they were in their faith, and so could their Rabbi.

I've found myself in many storms emotionally, relationally, even financially, and it can be a very disorienting experience. The pressure heightens and life squeezes what's really happening out of me. I've said some drastic things to myself in tough scenarios, like, "God hates me. He left me. He doesn't care." When I read that the disciples cry out to Jesus, "Don't you care if we die?" I feel human, even comforted.

God knew it was important that I could read about the disciples flipping out so I could see that humans confess in tension, and that's not necessarily a bad thing. Perhaps it's a gift. I believe that God heals us in tension. Perhaps storms are actually invitations to cross over to the other side of our fear, and tension can be a catalyst to a clear view.

What would happen if we caught those drastic things we say about ourselves and God that aren't true and repented? What if, in every storm of our lives, we could shed a layer of our false selves through humility? What if, when life squeezes us, we paid attention to what's happening in our hearts? The Father so perfectly orchestrates moments in our lives where we can grow and mature and change.

The beauty in it all: the disciples didn't get it. They missed the point. So, Jesus calmed the water and gave them another opportunity to see. He didn't kick anyone out of the family. He didn't punish them. Jesus embraced His disciples and kept moving toward them because He loved them deeply.

Prompt: Go find a quiet space with the Father. Invite His Spirit to show you where you are being invited to cross over. Write a short prayer that you can meditate on throughout the day that will remind you of His kindness and His invitation to understand His nature. Remember this: God is ready to help. He isn't cruel and His intention isn't to hurt you.

This is mine: "Father, I soften my heart toward you. I see that you are always for me and that you want the best for me. I repent for the lie that you've left me. I trade in the panic I feel over my life for the truth that you are a good Father calling me to come closer to your heart."

Haven, age eight

A DARE...
To Take Off Your Shoes

***writing and photograph
by MELISSA HELSER***

We drive and drive and search for a moment...a moment to be set free from the car's boundaries and run into the open glory of the Norwegian coutryside. My children love adventure. I guess all children love adventure, or at least those of us who dare to remain children do. We drive too long and tension rises—turning off the paved road onto gravel is risky business in the middle of nowhere. Long the road winds, down and down until suddenly we see open fields diving into mountain lakes, and the squeals of delight come and the running begins. At the lake's edge I see the sparkle in her eyes and I know exactly what she desires. With no hesitation I release a yes. She submerges her feet in the cold mountain water and is full.

Full to the brim.

There are truly seasons that require a moment of taking off shoes tight, and submerging released toes into the frigid water. Refreshment covers the soul from the bottom up.

I dare you to do something beyond your norm.
To search until you find it.
No matter how long it takes.
And when you come upon the beauty—
hold nothing back.

Take off your shoes.
Declare it a Holy Place.

WE BECOME FREE

RECIPE FOR RECEIVING HELP FROM OTHERS
by MOLLY KATE SKAGGS / *art by* JUSTINA STEVENS

"YOU, MY BROTHERS AND SISTERS, WERE CALLED TO BE FREE. BUT DO NOT USE YOUR FREEDOM TO INDULGE THE FLESH; RATHER, SERVE ONE ANOTHER HUMBLY IN LOVE." GALATIANS 5:13, NIV

One early autumn weekend, my friends and I were on a ministry trip in the beautiful North Carolina mountains. We had the privilege of pouring into the community of some dear friends of ours, and on Saturday we had the opportunity to enjoy a big breakfast together. After we prayed, I got in line, quickly filling my plate and coffee cup, then made my way toward the screen door so that I could sit on the porch. Both of my hands were full, so I tried pushing the door open with my shoulder. The spring was tighter than I expected, making the door very difficult to open. Suddenly, my great efforts resulted in me getting stuck with hot coffee spilling all over the floor and myself. Thankfully, I was not burned, but my pride was profoundly singed. In a word, I was humiliated and spent the next few seconds verbally chastising myself for being so ridiculous.

I glanced down at my side and saw one of our friends on his hands and knees with a fistful of paper towels. He was not saying anything, not laughing or hurling sarcastic remarks at me. He was quietly cleaning up my mess. Though very embarrassed, I willingly gave in to his help. "Thank you so much," I awkwardly said, trying to soften. He gave me a warm, silent smile as he handed me a paper towel for my coffee-stained arm.

Have you ever shouted so loud, either internally or outwardly, "Why do these things always happen to me?!" A couple of months later, I experienced another moment of embarrassment where I ended up punishing myself again for a simple mistake. In my fit, the Father brought back the memory from the mountain trip. Sometimes, it's really good to go back and sit in these kinds of moments with the Father and allow Him to give you eyes to see what was really going on. Though my pride swelled, I felt His heart reaching toward me. It was difficult, but I began to learn the process of going back into moments of shame and asking Him to teach me something. He showed me that although my desire to serve others is a lovely quality of my heart, it can easily become a ditch of self-righteousness that disconnects me from my own need for help. My embarrassment wasn't because I'd made a mistake; it was because my false image of being fine on my own had shattered loudly on the floor in front of everyone. The shame I felt for being needy was on display before the eyes it really mattered to the most: my own.

In the quiet space of my heart, I closed my tearful eyes, turned back to the Lord and repented. I love the Lord and how He doesn't treat disappointing moments like that with disgust or exasperation. He wanted to show me His heart for my shame: He was right there with me in the hands and feet of a brother who immediately jumped in to help me clean my mess. Although pride and self-hatred robbed me of being able to receive the gift the Father was offering me then, allowing Him to take me back to it taught me that shame could be an avenue where the Father would always meet me with love and understanding. Even in my most shameful moments, humility will always enable me to receive the fullness of Himself and His gifts for me. In moments of humiliation now, I am learning to interpret the message more accurately. Instead of *I'm so stupid, I can't believe I did that,* I am hearing, *That was really tough! Although I wish that hadn't happened, it did. Maybe I am trying too hard and need some help.* Humility carries a posture that says: "I am actually really limited in some areas, but so worthy of love, help and strength from other people!"

Maybe you are like me and have found it difficult to be seen in hard moments and to reach out for help. Maybe you have felt afraid that your vulnerability and weakness will be rejected, rather than pulled into love and acceptance. I am still on the road of humility, learning and growing in the gift of dependency on God through the love of others when I am the one who really needs it. But I am more confident in this truth: we become free when we allow shame to lead us to humility. And when we find Jesus and others waiting for us there, there is no longer a need to hold up the masks or false images. We become free to love and be loved, free to become more of who we actually are created to be: very delighted-in children of a very satisfied and loving Father.

Prompt: After reading this, do you recall a moment where you experienced overwhelming shame and punished yourself for needing help from others? Allow the Lord to take you back to the memory and ask Him, "Father, that was a hard moment! Will you show me your perspective and teach me something about how you were coming to set me free right then?" Journal His response and receive His gift of covering and love through those He has set around you.

HOW DO I PARTNER WITH GOD?

by GRAHAM COOKE / photograph by MORGAN CAMPBELL & JUSTINA STEVENS

In the very beginning of creation, the first words that God said about mankind in Genesis 1:26 (NASB) were, "Let Us make mankind in Our image, according to Our likeness…" He has been faithful to that process for thousands of years, and with countless millions of people. All the life situations and stories of people with God are constantly about becoming like God.

KEY 01
EVERYTHING GOD DOES IS RELATIONAL

He wanted a people who would be loved by Him and want to walk with Him in the course of life, so that they would become like Him. This is called "primary purpose" and His heart is still governed that way today. He is faithful to the process of our being made in His image.

A process is a series of steps that we take with Him as we learn to "grow up in all *aspects* into Him who is the head, that is, Christ" (Ephesians 4:15, NASB). We always need to root our learning in the nature of God. One of the most amazing things to know about God is that He is an absolute! He is absolutely unchanging! Here are two key verses upon which I have built my relationship with Him:

"For I, the Lord, do not change; therefore you, the sons of Jacob, are not consumed" (Malachi 3:6, NASB 1995).

"Jesus Christ is the same yesterday and today, and forever" (Hebrews 13:8, NASB).

I live with God between these two verses! I always know where I am with God because He does not change. He is the same toward me on a bad day as He is on my best day. He always does exactly what He says (see Numbers 23:19). He is constant in who He is as the Giver of all life (see James 1:17). The way He describes Himself in Scripture as our Rock, Fortress, High Tower and Cornerstone is to impart to us the strength of His love, purpose and integrity toward us. Personally, this is where I rest in Him. He loves me and all my circumstances too. Because Christ lives in me, all my circumstances are in Him also. All our circumstances are there for what we are learning about Him, about ourselves and about how He brings those two aspects into unity and oneness in Him.

Learning in the Kingdom is very different to learning from the world. It's like the world is playing baseball and the Kingdom is playing football. Different rules apply because there is a different methodology. The same applies to a religious, legalistic church world that uses shame, blame, condemnation and judgment as learning tools to avoid sin. When Jesus discipled people, He did so in the ways of love, grace and truth in relationship with His Father. Kingdom learning is always about transformation. It is primarily concerned with the original intent of making people in Christ's image and according to His likeness (see Genesis 1:26). Therefore, all our learning is relational both in the context of your current life situation, and in the context of who God wants you to become now and next. What you perceive God wants to be for you will drive everything in your life.

This means that in Kingdom learning, God is concerned with your personal development and also with an outcome in your life situation. In a troubled and problematic world the issue *is* the issue! We want a resolution of our circumstances, and a solution to the problem. We want rescue, "I'm a Christian, get me out of here!"

In the Kingdom of relationship, the purpose is our transformation into God's image and then our situation can be changed to fit who we are becoming. At times, He works both together, of course. At other times He wants change in you as a priority. So, for example, if a life situation is producing anxiety in you, He will want to exchange anxiety for peace. If we do not allow that to happen, anxiety will govern the issue and we may not see any resolution. Anxiety unchecked can produce apprehension, tension, stress and fretfulness. Problems can grow if we do not see that becoming like Jesus is the primary part of the situation changing in His favor. This is where God teaches us His ways, His truth and His lifestyle in our circumstances. In Jesus this becomes our stance in the circumstance.

KEY 02
USE QUESTIONS IN ORDER TO ENGAGE WITH GOD

Relational learning is really about the miracle of personal change that God wants to bring into your situation because of the circumstances that are present. The process is how He creates a partnership in the way of change so that we can cooperate with Him no matter what is going on in our life. And a key part of that process is the questions that we get to ask Him.

Two of my favorite questions that drive the process of becoming are both found on the Day of Pentecost in Acts 2. The first is, "What does this mean?" (see Acts 2:12) This is a *relational* question.

"Lord, what does this situation mean for you and me?"
"How will this situation empower me to become like you?"
"What do you want to change in my character?"
"What aspect of your nature are you creating in me now?"

These are a few of the questions I ask the Lord because I know that He will never waste an opportunity to create another layer and level of His image in me. He does not create difficult circumstances so that He can change me, but He knows how to take advantage of what is in opposition to us.

The second question in Acts 2:37 is, "What must I do?" This is a *partnership* question. We are always engaged with God. "How do I partner with you to enable your purpose to be realized?" It is an exploring question about how we are going to learn to walk with God because of this situation! I am expecting some growth to occur so that I can grow in spirit and truth. Remember that every situation is not just about a resolution of the situation, that is a functional response only. If we fail to grow and change then we guarantee that this situation will come around again and again!

Never ask the "why" question. "Why me? Why this? Why now?" The "why" question seldom gets answered on earth. It is a victim question. Jesus in you is not a victim ever! He is more than a conqueror residing in you. Being in Him empowers you to victory and overcoming as you learn His power in a relational way.

There are three aspects of change that are always a part of your learning in Jesus. Firstly, He is going to change your perspective on how the circumstances look to the Father. He will give you a new lens to create a new vision. You will learn to see a situation the way God sees it. Ask this question: "If Jesus was looking out through my eyes, how would He see this situation, this person, this difficulty? How would the Holy Spirit turn this problem into His opportunity?"

Secondly, He will upgrade your thinking in line with what you are now seeing! He wants to create a mindset in you that is not focused on the problem. The mind set on the negative (i.e. flesh) is hostile to God, it cannot grow in Christ or please God. The mind set on the Spirit creates life and peace. If God's Spirit lives in you then you are alive to all His possibilities. He gives life to you regardless of circumstances. I love Romans 8:16-17; read it in The Passion Translation. Father, Son and Spirit have a Kingdom approach to life that is extremely different from a troubled world. As your mind in Christ is being renewed, your language will adjust to the Kingdom perspective so that you can speak about circumstances in the language of God.

Developing your new lens, mindset and language are a part of every situation. As you learn the process, these aspects become more powerful and more of a constant part of your walk in Christ. This means that you would pray about situations in the same language as Jesus. You would confess what He is declaring to you. Asking questions allows you to refocus from the world to the Kingdom.

THIS IS MY CRAFTED PRAYER IN SUCH MOMENTS:

"FATHER, WOULD YOU MULTIPLY GRACE AND PEACE TO ME SO THAT I CAN LEARN, IN REAL TIME, IN THE WAY THAT SUITS YOUR NATURE AND EMPOWERS MY TRUST IN YOUR KINDNESS TO ME?

EMPOWER ME LORD, TO KNOW YOUR WAYS AND LEARN YOUR TRUTH. TOUCH MY LENS, THINKING AND LANGUAGE SO THAT I CONFORM TO YOUR WILL AND YOUR WAY.

FATHER, I KNOW YOU ARE MAKING ME IN YOUR IMAGE AND ACCORDING TO YOUR LIKENESS. THANK YOU FOR THIS OPPORTUNITY TO WALK WITH YOU IN A NEW WAY, AMEN."

Life situations can vary in terms of difficulty and also length of time; from one day to several, from a week to a few weeks or longer.

Being in this process with God will be the making of you. You will need at some point to learn some patience, perseverance and joy in the process. Grace means that if you fail this test, you will be given another opportunity to take it again...because God will never leave you, nor will He fail you. Learning is always repeated until we get it! Learning comes with a test. This particular Scripture has always meant such a lot to me.

James 1:2-4 (NASB), "Consider it all joy...when you encounter various trials, knowing that the testing of your faith produces endurance. And let endurance have its perfect result, so that you may be perfect and complete, lacking nothing." This verse tells us we can become fully mature in Jesus. This is a perfect description of a good lens creating a great way of thinking and producing a language that really works!

Never forget that Christ is in you! You and He are partners in all circumstances. He is your Redeemer in everything. We get saved once and we live redeemed every day. "...it is God who is at work in you both to will and to work for His good pleasure" (Philippians 2:13, NASB).

Asking God questions has been one of the constant and continuous joys of my life. Keep a notebook handy for the answers.

Our home is built

Medallion yellow bees winning my trust
What sacred wisdom must be circulating
as they plunge headfirst into the blossoms
When they murmur into my ear
I'm learning
to listen
for their glazed secrets
Thank you for the yellow blooms
On the dresser

Tuscan yellow ribbons of sky do jazz hands
around the sun as she kisses
tops of trees in her everlasting goodbye
and hello to the world

Parchment yellow blueberry insides
who wait
for the lowly mouth
that takes a small enough bite to notice them

photography by MORGAN CAMPBELL and SYDNEE MELA

with yellow
by MARY HALL

Yellow healing balm
On longing desert yellow palms
Reverence is unearthed
in tending to skin—humankind's covering

Citrus is my orchard's aroma
Last year's oranges
This year's canary yellow lemons
What if my heart's well tastes like lemon water
to You?

Quilt yellow speckles set on a timber turtle shell
On her leisurely dip
She lifts her head above water to remind me
that You will not leave me behind

Lantern yellow light to my feet
Kingdom yellow sight when we meet
And on golden yellow streets will I dance forever

HE DIDN'T HIDE HIMSELF

WHY DOES BEAUTY MATTER?
writing and art by JUSTINA STEVENS

Why did God create thousands of variations of flowers in rainbow colors? Or labor over how light and shadow play together? Why so much time on hair textures and the way they respond to invisible breeze? Why glowing lights in the sky, and a moon that waxes and wanes?

Isn't it amazing that God didn't reserve beauty for the saved? It would be a great deal, don't you think? If you accept Jesus as your Lord and Savior you get to see constellations in the sky, leaves changing fire-red in autumn and bees buzzing that create thick golden honey for your tea and biscuits… It would have been a great business strategy. Everyone would buy in, because at the end of the day, we are all moved by beauty. We crave a full-color life. But God gave beauty freely to all humanity. He doesn't reserve a sunset for the sinless. In fact, He calls to His lost children through brilliant light and high mountain peaks. He whispers to the downcast through gently falling snow. I believe God knew beauty would lead us to questions that need to be asked; He knew the conversation it would initiate.

God didn't and doesn't hide from us, because just as He is Love, He is also Beauty. In a miraculously generous way, Beauty is still making Himself clear and obvious to those who are willing to seek Him.

Once, when I was at a museum, I saw a painting that stopped me in my tracks. A large scale abstract piece with a blush-peach stroke on top and what looked like several deep, muddled colors seeping out from behind it. Because I've practiced being moved by beauty, it was clear to me that I needed to stay there. A quietness washed over me: the sensation of curiosity rising from my soul without any words. Then finally a clear question arose from my soul, "What are you doing here?" Was it the painting asking me or me asking the painting? Honestly, I didn't know. But I leaned in.

I've learned that judging art and beauty is a silly pastime. A much simpler thing to do is make space for beauty to be seen and minister to me. I am an artist myself, and I've practiced not being afraid of what art may stir up in my heart. If the fruit of looking at an abstract painting is darkness, heaviness or despair, I simply move on. It isn't my place to judge the maker of the work—who knows what pain they had to endure to generate their piece? My job as a human is to carefully receive, and in this moment with the large peach painting, I was experiencing more than just curiosity. I could feel the presence of God—as if His face was hidden in the strokes, His eyes locked on mine. "What are you doing here?" again washed over me. Tears welled up in my eyes. *What's happening?* I thought to myself, but I wasn't going to run from the conversation. I let the tears stream down my face, and I took a deep breath. I stepped toward the painting's description to read about its creator: a woman, Helen Frankenthaler, someone I had studied and admired in college. "You belong here," I heard the Father say. And in this simple exchange of curiosity and words, I realized how God was using beauty to dig down deep into my soul.

At this specific point in my life, I was trying to figure out if I was going to dare to venture into the world of abstract art. I'd say things like: Why give people reason to misunderstand me? Why confuse people? I studied the human form in school so I could make pieces that make sense! I used these excuses to push down my heart's desire. In this moment at the museum, God challenged my assumptions about myself and others and opened a door for me to try. In this simple moment, beauty changed my mind. I do not regret lingering that day.

We have woven photography, poetry, prose and art through this book because our community has found the Healer, the Helper and the Redeemer in beauty. And so,

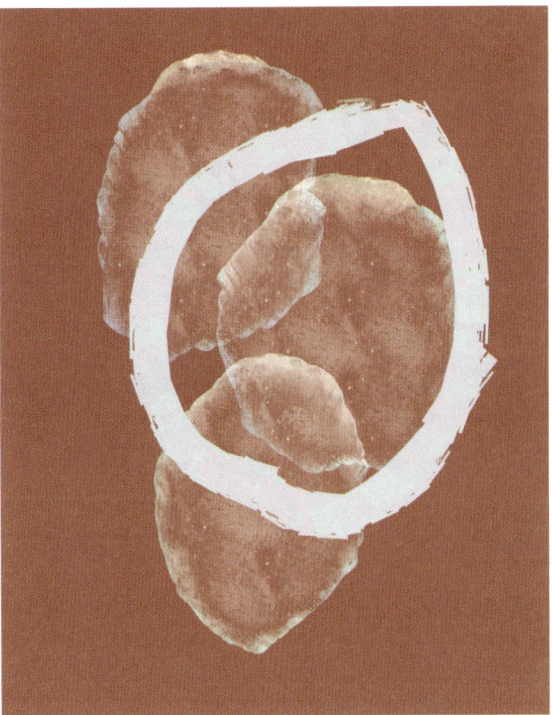

we have created space for you to practice being impacted by this special part of God. We charge you to not skip the beauty, but to commune with God in it. Embrace the uncomfortable silence or stillness it asks for. Allow it to call to the depths of who you are. Do not reject this sacred part of God.

Prompt: Today, pray this prayer: "God, I make space for beauty in my life. I open my hands and make space for the Creator of the heavens and earth to move me in the simplicity and majesty of creation. Father, will you open my eyes today to linger a bit more with you?"

MY LIFE IS WEATHERED AND SOMETIMES ADRIFT. I DON'T ALWAYS KNOW WHERE I AM GOING. I RESIST CONFUSION AND SELF-JUDGMENT; I SURVEY MY COLORS AND TAKE IN MY EVER-CHANGING APPEARANCE. I FIND PEACE WITH WHERE I HAVE BEEN AND RECEIVE THE LONGING FOR WHERE I AM GOING.

writing and photograph by MELISSA HELSER

the PAIN of a FRUITLESS GARDEN

RECIPE ON REFLECTION AND ASKING GOD FOR HELP
by JESSIE MILLER / photograph by MORGAN CAMPBELL

It is painful to do fruitless work. The discouragement that comes after putting in large amounts of effort with little to no yield drives many to quit things they once loved. We resign from people, tasks, dreams and most sadly, our faith, because we feel hopeless. *What's the point?* Most of us want to find some answer, some quick fix for why things are not responding how we had hoped they would. And all of us seem to have a threshold of how many times we will continue to try at something without feeling successful. The reality is that this is happening daily in the lives of believers when it comes to their walk with God. Even you might be hitting a threshold. *Does God really care about me? Are these boundaries really leading to my good? Does God's way really work? Is it all worth it?*

If you feel distant, disillusioned, frustrated, angry, heartbroken or simply discouraged about how your walk with the Lord feels, you are not alone. But take heart, your questions are a sign that you're awake and hungry to be full of passion and fruit. Your questions should lead you to better work—not to less work or even the same work. There are so many things to learn about how to actually connect with God in a way that, over time, will yield the fruit He promises. He is not withholding good from you or waiting for you to get things just right to come through. He has not forgotten about you. He is not a god waiting for a rain dance and then selfishly deciding if He is pleased enough to let it pour. He longs to bring forth His Spirit in your life, but we must tend to the soil in which His love grows. There is work that comes with maturing in God. The good news it that He longs to do this work with us. He is ready to lend us His strength in our weakness, His understanding in our frustration and His company in our loneliness. He longs to share the joy of celebration over all that will eventually come when we stay the course.

If you're looking for magic formulas and simple self-help hacks, you will be disappointed. Although some of our healing and growth is quick, maturity takes time. There is no way around working out our salvation, and it is so important that we feel equipped to do the right work. Our hearts are like a garden. The Gospel reveals to us the worth of our hearts to the Father, regardless of their current states, and fills us with the hope that under our good Gardener's care, new things can grow. We are offered abundant life. Although there is a miracle that we receive, fruit does not come as quickly or as painlessly as most would wish. This is the call of discipleship—to go beyond simply teaching one another what to believe, and instead, teach the practices that will help right beliefs fully take root. The garden of our hearts cannot simply have a flower bed "For Jesus." We must learn how to interact with Him in the entirety of our garden and we need to learn tools that help us till the soil, tend the seeds, address the weeds and prune. This is the work that leads to a fruitful life.

Prompt: Where are you in pain, friend? Are you discouraged? Are you weary? Are you angry? Close your eyes and picture the garden of your heart—kneel at the part of the land where you feel resentment for the lack of yield. Cry out to God. Give Him your frustration, your tears, your anger, your hopelessness and ask Him to come. Repent for your pride, your hurry and your demands. Ask Him to come be with you, to teach you how to tend the soil and to fill you with courage to endure. Stay in the moment until you feel His closeness. Breathe in breaths of hope. There is work to be done, but there is fruit to come.

YOUR THOUGHTS DEFINE ME

Haven, age six

RECIPE FOR SONSHIP / by JONATHAN DAVID HELSER / photograph by GINNY CORBETT

> "HOW PRECIOUS TO ME ARE YOUR THOUGHTS, GOD! HOW VAST IS THE SUM OF THEM! WERE I TO COUNT THEM, THEY WOULD OUTNUMBER THE GRAINS OF SAND—WHEN I AWAKE, I AM STILL WITH YOU." PSALM 139:17-18, NIV

I had this amazing experience one day after Melissa took my little daughter, Haven, shopping for the first time. She let Haven pick out her own dress. When they returned, I was in my room reading in my favorite chair. I heard my little girl's feet run up the stairs to her room above me. I could tell by the commotion that she was either wrestling an alligator, or that she was furiously changing into her new clothes. Then I heard her little feet come back down the stairs, and she burst into my room. Without any words she ran up and stopped in front of me, wearing a new dress she had picked out. This was one of those moments when time seemed to stop. She stood still and time stood still. I realized it was one of the greatest moments I would ever have as a father. She was waiting to be defined by my voice. Her little heart was like clay, waiting on my thoughts to shape her. With everything inside of me I looked deep into her eyes and said, "Haven, you look more beautiful right now than you have in your whole life." Each day for the next week, Haven would put on her new dress and come find me. No matter what I was doing, she would pause before me and wait for my voice to tell her again that she was beautiful. It was like her little heart was saying over and over to me, "Do it again, Daddy...tell me who I am."

Identity is discovered through the voice we listen to. We have all been created to be defined by a Father's voice. Every girl is made to hear the words, "You are beautiful," and every boy is designed to hear the words, "Well done!"

My words over Haven are but a shadow of the radiant thoughts that the Father in Heaven has for her. Until we each have an encounter with our Father in Heaven, like my daughter had with me, we will spend our lives broken and in search of our identity.

Prompt: Go and find a quiet space and spend a few minutes getting still and relaxed. Pray this prayer out loud a few times until your heart begins to resonate with His love. This prayer is like going to the dressing room of Heaven and putting on the gift Jesus bought for you. Pray: "God, you so loved me that you bankrupted Heaven and gave your only Son to give me abundant life. Holy Spirit, I raise my hands to you like a child, and ask that you take off any of my old rags of fear, shame and guilt. Clothe me with the Father's tangible affections. I confess that I am no longer a sinner; I am a child redeemed by love. I wear a robe of righteousness on the inside and outside. I am in right standing with God. I am a fearless child, you are a very happy Father."

Speak this Scripture out loud a few times: "Let us then approach God's throne of grace with confidence, so that we may receive mercy and find grace to help us in our time of need" (Hebrews 4:16, NIV).

Picture yourself opening the door to the Father's room. Remember the Father is waiting on you with joyful expectation, so don't be afraid to approach His presence. Stand before His throne of grace as Haven stood before me and ask with brave confidence, "Daddy, what are your thoughts about me?"

Now pick up your journal and write with faith the thoughts you hear your Father speaking.

the WELL

I HAD COME TO THIS PLACE MANY TIMES BEFORE. I DIDN'T SPEAK THE LANGUAGE, BUT THE WATER WAS REFRESHING. SOMEHOW I UNDERSTOOD. THIRSTY PEOPLE HAVE A LOT IN COMMON. EVERYONE UNDERSTANDS WHAT THE WATER HAS TO SAY.

Here the old men don't work during the high heat. They are wise and wear cotton shirts to cool themselves in the breeze. Their wells run the deepest. They spend their afternoons under the willows braiding rope for the ends of their buckets. Should you taste of their wells, you would swear it was the sweetest water. One sip could quench your thirst. A full glass would spoil you forever for city water.

Here the old men say a man can gain all the water he'll drink in a lifetime if he's willing to dig. Their hands hold calluses acquired from a lifetime of digging. Just feel their handshakes. They will tell you the story of their sacrifice, seasons of back-breaking work dedicated to the sweetness found underground. Look at the young men and their eager hands. They admire the sacrifice of the old men. They have tasted and do not hesitate in giving their hearts to gain a lifetime of cool, refreshing water.

Pilgrims bring their thirst from far away. They arrive and find the shovel to be a rather uncomplicated tool. Digging is a simple job. They come with a plethora of canteens and buckets. They try to accumulate as much of the water as possible, but the high heat is vicious. Accumulated water evaporates quickly, and the water that's left goes stale. Every newcomer gets a taste but not all see the goodness. Many pilgrims come in a state of exhaustion and gulp the water, never tasting a thing. To them, the thought of endless digging for the whole course of their lives, seems like some sort of cruel joke and they never liberate what lies beneath their feet.

I was once a pilgrim. I gulped and choked and accumulated the water. I was driven by my thirst, with little ability to taste. But the locals were patient with me and taught me to sip the water. They taught me to listen to the cold sensation in my chest, to wait till it reaches thirsts I did not know I had. Now I spend my days tending my own well. The water was a lot murkier once, but I've shoveled my share of mud. Some may say spending hours a day knee-deep in mud is no way to live, but the only way to dig a well is through the mire.

I have found satisfaction in the water of my well. My well sustains me and I have access to the lifetime of treasure beneath my feet. Maybe one day, the young men will shake hands with me and learn the story of my sacrifice.

by JD GRAVITT
photography by GABRIEL RAMIREZ

LEARNING to HEAR

RECIPE ON LEARNING TO HEAR THE VOICE OF THE LORD

by PHYLLIS UNKEFER / *art by* JUSTINA STEVENS

It's a peculiar thing to hold conversation with Someone invisible. It takes a certain amount of daring, perhaps as much as it would take to step on the surface of a lake and expect to walk. More than once, I've felt confronted by it. It just doesn't always follow logic, feels questionable sometimes, irrational even and yet, I've found it to be as natural and quiet and familiar as breathing. The part of me that likes tangible things—like sitting at tables, holding hands when we pray, studying expressions that flash across faces—might prefer a different arrangement. Something a little more visible, a little more audible. But somehow the subtlest force in the universe, the Lord's still small voice, is also the most tremendous. The most extraordinary and impactful and real. My life has been deeply transformed by a God who speaks to me.

Maybe it was obvious that I'd come to love hearing the Lord's voice the day a block of snow fell from the top of a telephone line, exquisitely timed, to land directly on my nine-year-old head as I trudged along the sidewalk below. Back then, I knew next to nothing about the Holy Spirit, had never heard of the practice of listening to God. But in that moment, I exploded into the air, arms raised, leaping with instantaneous delight at the notion that erupted in my heart: God sees me! God sees me! Even me. When I was nine, Jesus spoke to me through the snow.

When I was eighteen, He spoke to me on a garden bench. That afternoon, I sat there agonized. I'd been chased by several years of depression and this anguished uncertainty at whether God existed. And I had nothing left in that moment but my humility. I told Jesus I didn't know if He was real, but I'd give my life to Him, I just needed Him to help me. His answer was wordless and stunningly immediate: waves of love suddenly poured over me like He'd tipped a jar of warm water right through me. His presence drenched all the way to my bones. With affection, He gathered my mind back together and permeated everything with relief. I couldn't shake the joy for months.

If you hear a voice like that, it's hard to ever lose fascination with it. After the garden bench, I read the Bible ravenously, listening for Him inside the words. And when somebody handed me a book about learning to hear His voice, I finished it in a matter of days. I had no idea what to do with the stories it told of the Holy Spirit speaking, in all His creative and clever ways, except to feel provoked. So I prayed over and over for weeks, "Lord, speak to me. Speak to me."

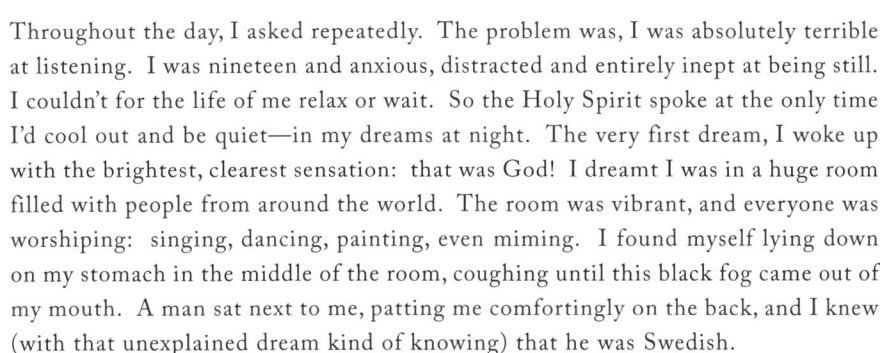

Throughout the day, I asked repeatedly. The problem was, I was absolutely terrible at listening. I was nineteen and anxious, distracted and entirely inept at being still. I couldn't for the life of me relax or wait. So the Holy Spirit spoke at the only time I'd cool out and be quiet—in my dreams at night. The very first dream, I woke up with the brightest, clearest sensation: that was God! I dreamt I was in a huge room filled with people from around the world. The room was vibrant, and everyone was worshiping: singing, dancing, painting, even miming. I found myself lying down on my stomach in the middle of the room, coughing until this black fog came out of my mouth. A man sat next to me, patting me comfortingly on the back, and I knew (with that unexplained dream kind of knowing) that he was Swedish.

Dreams are wild! And so vividly symbolic. Because Jesus is *still* speaking through parables. A week later, I recounted the dream to a friend. She didn't even hesitate to say, "I feel like I know what it means," she went on, "I know worship is a significant part of you and I sense that throughout your life, you'll end up worshiping with people all around the world [since then, this has come true]. You laid on your stomach coughing because Jesus is going to take you through a season of deep healing [this has also come true]. And the Swedish man next to you, patting you on the back, he is going to send you into ministry." Now, do I recommend that we hand out weighty interpretations of dreams hastily? Not necessarily. But I was not at all upset about it a year later when I sat in a discipleship school classroom and the director stopped in the middle of his teaching, for some unexplained reason, to announce, "I am 100% Swedish." He sent me out on outreach a month later, and I was in ministry under his leadership for the following five years. Before I even knew how to listen, Jesus spoke to me through dreams (and through friends who honor dreams).

The truth is, the Father wasn't all that worried about how bad I was at listening. When there's hunger in my soul to hear Him (and at times, even when there's not), He's convinced of His ability to get through to me. But still in His commitment to my thriving, He wasn't down to let me stay there. I once heard a teacher pose the question, "Do you know why the Lord speaks so softly?" My classmates and I offered up our mumbled speculations, but the question was semi-rhetorical and he went on to tell us, "He speaks softly so that if we desire to hear Him, we have to come close. And that's what He wants most." There's not much reason to draw near to someone who's shouting; you can hear them from up the street. Instead, we've been asked to rely on the weightlessness of a whisper. Just so that we'll draw intimately close.

And for me, this is where the confrontation lies. Setting out to be still has, over and over, forced me to face the state of my own heart. Especially, the state of my trust. When I was nineteen, I struggled to trust. My mind felt nebulous whenever I listened, like it was overcast with a thick haze of doubt. But hearing God takes trust. A trust that's more subtle but just as courageous as swinging our legs over the edge of a boat and expecting to walk on the waves. The beautiful thing is, the Father will build trust with us. He's *that* humble. He'll do it in a string of moments. Not by demand or our willful attempts to force it. And to be honest, it still surprises me that one of the sharpest pathways into trust between He and I has been vulnerability.

This was clear one day through some of my less articulated honesty when I was out hiking, still age nineteen. That afternoon, a yellow butterfly moseyed past my shoulder, and I spontaneously dared the Lord, "You could make that butterfly land on my arm if you want." I had not stopped craving connection with Jesus and I expressed my desire for Him without saying it in any remotely vulnerable terms, but the longing was still there. I brushed the thought away abruptly, not wanting to "test" the Lord. But two weeks later, my hesitation folded under the paper-ish wings of a black and yellow butterfly that landed on my sleeve. I was reading outside at a picnic table when it landed. Its ornateness enthralled me, until I was deeply distracted from all my distrust and I was entirely still. That's when I heard, for the first time, the Father's thoughts stream into my mind. He said my name with warmth, "Phyllis," and immediately had my attention, "Do you see this butterfly? I know everywhere it flies and every place it's landed. Do you see its thread-like legs? They're fragile, they could easily break. But for as long as this butterfly has been alive, I've protected its legs. I've watched over them and kept them. If I care this much about a butterfly, how much more do I care about you?" (It sounded like something I'd heard before about sparrows.) The next moment, the butterfly lifted off my sleeve and landed on my back. But I didn't want it to stay there, so I shook my shoulders until it flew back onto my hand. The Lord continued, "Daughter, in the same way that you didn't like the butterfly resting on your back, you don't like when you can't hear or see me. But a butterfly on your back will never harm you. And neither will I. Unlike the idle butterfly, I will keep protecting and caring for you."

Suffice it to say, I was shook. When the butterfly finally flew away, I could only sit there and breathe. I probably smiled too, for reasons that passing strangers wouldn't have imagined. In my practice over the years, I have come to know that God speaks tenderly. With kindness and affection. He also speaks with playfulness, clarity and sternness when needed. But He set the tone for me first with His kindness. This became even clearer to me some months later. After weeks of unhearing frustration, I finally chose the path of vulnerability again. I asked my leaders and friends to pray for me and my struggle to trust. I don't know how long I waited and prayed. But I do remember the morning that things took a turn. During prayer, I closed my eyes, risked hopefulness and listened. A few moments came and went, but then I saw it. So briefly and fleetingly, a picture in my mind. It was the image of a torn piece of fabric and a sewing needle steadily stitching it back up. I knew, with that unexplained knowing, that the fabric was my life, and the needle and stitch were God's promise to restore me. I remember gasping at how easily the picture slipped into my mind, how recognizable and simple it was. And it became apparent to me then: it's not hard to hear God. When I calm down and wait, He will make Himself generously clear.

Since then, I'd like to say that I've never felt uncertain again. But that's not usually how things go. I can say that I've come to love listening to His voice. It's not always as dramatic as visitations from butterflies; it feels more like the daily talk of friends. Years later, our conversations have taught me more of what He's like: no one is as lavishly affectionate as the Lord. He delights to articulate His love. I'll ask Him a question, and frequently His answer is to talk about how He adores me (which is not usually what I'm trying to hear, but it's the truer answer to my question). He speaks to so many things—guidance, wisdom, correction, conviction and so on—but at the center of it all, He wants to restore my sense of His heart. Jesus has shown me His heart through every time I've heard Him, through this string of quiet and surprising moments. And when I know His heart, it overturns my distrust. My fears do resurface occasionally, but I just get vulnerable again. Like a couple years ago when I didn't think I was hearing the Lord very clearly and I told Him so. As honestly as I could. He spoke these words directly to my mind, "Every time you put pen to paper and journal my voice, you are offering me your mustard seed of faith. I will always answer your mustard seed of faith." This one thought settled something inside me. If faith is what pleases Him, then anytime I attempt to listen, I've already delighted His heart. So I choose to keep giving my mustard seed, trusting His willingness, believing that He can reach me. And His words somehow become the water where I can walk.

Prompt: Open up your heart in vulnerability before the Lord. Be honest with the Lord about one thing that makes you nervous when it comes to hearing His voice and let Him respond to it.

ARE YOU ENJOYING GOD?

RECIPE FOR RELATIONSHIP WITH GOD

I spotted her in the college chapel sitting alone, cynically gazing at those gathered around the altar celebrating the goodness of God. They were experiencing revival, she wasn't. Curious about her pain, I moved to sit beside her. I decided to let her speak first, so we sat a long time…until suddenly she burst out angrily, "It just doesn't work!"

She folded her arms in disgust and went on to explain how she had become a Christian. She had given her heart to Jesus and gotten saved, then proceeded to faithfully do all she was instructed to do. She went to church three times a week. Religiously. She read her Bible and memorized Scripture every day. She prayed, tithed and witnessed to the lost, but then confessed, "I have never felt further from God in my whole life. Look how happy they are, and me? I'm miserable. Why don't I enjoy God anymore?" Before I could even close my eyes to pray I heard God say, "In everything she's doing, she's trying to buy relationship with me by her good deeds. Tell her to quit working for my love."

She was shocked when I told her to put away her Bible, and quit going to church. I suggested she spend her tithe on herself, and advised her to quit witnessing, for what kind of witness was she if she wasn't happy in God? She drew away from me, and said indignantly, "Why should I quit all those things if I want to be a Christian?" I replied, "Because you are using them to work for God's love and that does not work!" She stared at me and I could see her eyes were holding back tears. Then she turned and buried her head on my shoulder and cried, "But how do I do that? How do I let Him love me?"

It is amazing how quickly we can religiously shift from the prodigal son being loved on by God, to the elder brother doing all the right things for God but missing the party. Or we can move from sitting at the feet of Jesus like Mary in adoring worship, to taking on the Martha spirit that was distracted from enjoying Jesus, thinking she had to work for Him. I prayed with the frustrated girl that sat alone in the pew of the student chapel, "O Lord, forgive us for thinking we must do something to achieve your acceptance of us, while all the time you are asking us to come to you and let you love us into loving you back."

Over the past fifty years of following the man of Galilee, I have returned over and over to this reality: How do I live a life of enjoying God? By giving myself to Him for Him to enjoy me!

Prompt: Pray this prayer: "God, I open up my heart and surrender to your love. I let you love me first, and I let go of my need to prove my worth to you. I rest in the fact that you see me, every part, and you call me worthy of the Cross, of your perfect Son. What is one way I can enjoy you in this season?" Be still and let Him speak. Journal His response to you.

by KEN HELSER

the WIND & the RAIN

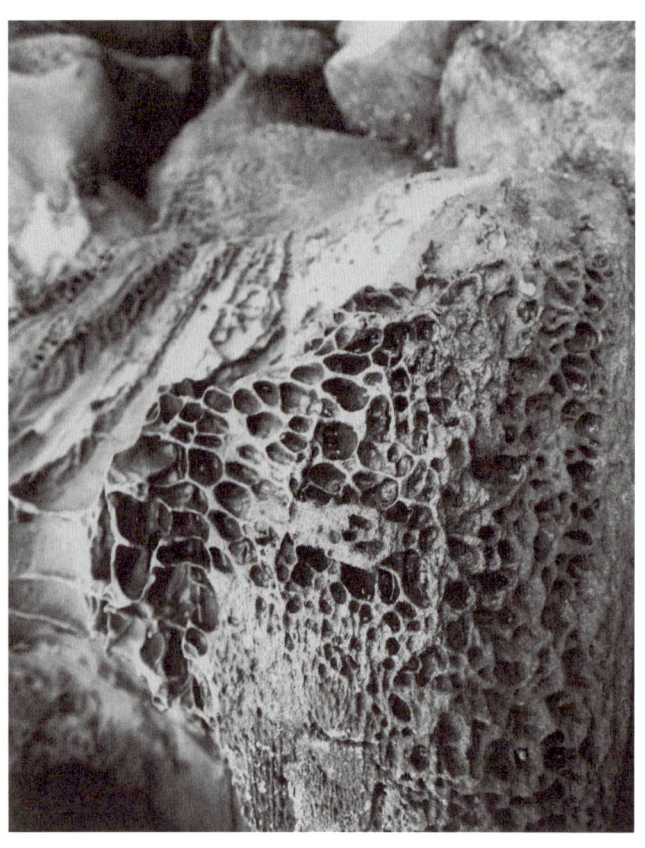

IT IS HERE IN THE QUIET I PAUSE AND SEE THAT THE WIND AND THE RAIN HAVE PRESSED ME ON EVERY SIDE, AND YET IN MY PRESSING YOU HAVE MADE BEAUTY.

I believe there are moments in life where the Holy Spirit invites us to pause and reflect on the seasons past. So much of our life is spent running from moment to moment, never stopping to look around us or look back. We are often afraid to stop. Afraid to see and breathe in the reality of seasons gone, and yet we yearn for the silence. I am learning that my yearning to stop is the Holy Spirit leading me into reflection of the beauty in my seasons gone. He woos me into seeing what He sees and leads me to let go of insecurities and fears, inviting me to pick up a new perspective. He woos me and asks me to exchange what I think is there for what is really there, that I may see the beauty in the pressing.

I have stood on the shores of many oceans. I have marveled at the glory of the water and majesty of the sky and the way they kiss each other. I have stood with the wind in my face and sand surrounding my toes. I have breathed in the salt air and thanked God for His brilliant creation. I have walked miles upon miles along beaches all over the world. In the walking, I found things that marked my heart, treasures that I picked up and stored in the pockets of my memory. These glorious rocks are etched in my memory as moments where I thanked God for the wind and the rain and the way they shaped every line and divot. In reflection, I am learning to thank God for seemingly meaningless things. It is in the thanking that I breathe in the glory of the Master's hand and understand that when I thought He had stopped carving, He had just begun.

writing and photography by MELISSA HELSER

A SIMPLE QUESTION

RECIPE ON THE PLAYFULNESS OF GOD

by ALLIE SAMPSON

In my early twenties, I was in a major season of self-discovery. Up until that point I'd felt so disconnected from my own heart, and not knowing myself had become a huge obstacle to knowing God. A lack of self-awareness meant I could not connect to the Father in whose image I was made, the Christ who was in me (the hope of glory) or the indwelling Holy Spirit. Disconnection from my own heart left me feeling disconnected from God, and I struggled to figure out how to begin getting to know myself. But in His kindness, God seemed to sneak moments of self-discovery into every part of my normal, daily life.

One late-February evening, I made my way up my long driveway tired but satisfied. It had been a full day of balancing work, classes and friendship, and I was ready to unwind. Making a point to slow down, I paused on the front porch and stared out into the tree-line in front of me. I took a deep breath. And that's when I heard it. A spontaneous question leapt up from my heart and tumbled out of my mouth: "God, if I were a tree, what kind of tree would I be?" I was caught off guard by my own question. Before I even had time to second-guess myself, I heard Him say, "Silver birch."

I laughed out loud, surprised twice-over. I'd never anticipated asking God something so random, and at that time in my life, I would have told you God didn't answer trivial questions like the one I'd just asked. In my perspective, God was too busy, too serious, too sovereign to answer the low-stakes questions of distracted daydreamers. I was shocked by how quickly He'd answered me and was overwhelmed with curiosity. I'd never heard of a silver birch tree, and that exciting reality was evidence that I couldn't have possibly made up what I'd heard.

I spent the next several weeks researching silver birch trees: sifting through forestry websites and gardening blogs, searching for qualities, facts and data about this name I'd been given. I was astonished by what I found. Not only did silver birch trees exist, but they had fascinating attributes that directly lined up with other things God had been speaking to me about. I was blown away that this tree had some of the exact same qualities that the Father had been telling me were a part of my own nature: the ability to grow after devastation, an unstoppable drive to find Water, a reliable tendency to provide shade for trees that take more time to establish and grow.

He was affirming me—speaking to me about me—and I felt remarkably understood.

For the next eight months, birch trees seemed to be everywhere. They showed up in novels I was reading, on covers of poetry books, in songs playing in my favorite stores while shopping. I couldn't contain my smile, or my tears, as I whispered simple prayers: "You know me. You understand me. Thank you." My desire to understand myself was even more important to Him than it was to me.

I am grateful for this moment—for the simple question that leapt up from the playful places in my heart and how the Father stepped in before I had a chance to discredit the question or label it as "too ridiculous." The Lord met me in my playful nature, and it changed everything. Now I give myself space to ask the silly questions, confident that He created and loves every part of me—especially the parts that are childlike, joyful and trusting. That question led to a season of me feeling more inspired than I'd ever been before. It led me to writing songs and poems, to confidence and joy, to more questions and more answers. It led to a belief that I am understood.

Prompt: Have you limited God's voice to only the serious areas of your life? When was the last time you asked Him a question, just to see what He says? Think of a silly question you could ask God about yourself, and then ask Him with confidence. It could be anything. If you're having a hard time coming up with an idea, feel free to borrow my question: "God, if I were a tree, what kind of tree would I be?" Practice courage and don't disqualify the moment. Listen to what He says and journal His voice. Then, do some research and invite the Holy Spirit to help you understand why He thinks of you this way. Savor the feeling of being understood.

BREATH PRAYER

by JONATHAN DAVID HELSER

By the time you finish reading this writing you will have taken around sixty breaths. Before you close your eyes tonight and go to sleep, you will have breathed around 20,000 times, and by the end of this year your lungs will have inhaled and exhaled around 8,030,000 times. It is incredible that you did all this without even thinking about it or even really trying that hard to do it, yet it is this quiet and constant rhythm that has kept you alive each day and each year.

A few years ago some friends of ours spent a weekend with us at our home. We nearly spent every moment of that weekend together, and as our time was coming to a close, one of our friends pointed out something he had observed about Melissa. He said to her, "Did you know that I heard you quietly say, 'Thank you, Jesus,' dozens and dozens of times this weekend?" He was deeply inspired by this rhythm, and it surprised Melissa because she didn't even realize she was doing it so much. Just like our lungs breathing in the air, this short prayer of gratitude was maintaining Melissa's connection to the Lord and bringing life to her soul. The monks and mystics would call a prayer like this a "breath prayer." A breath prayer is a short, simple sentence that can be said in one breath, and prayed throughout the day. I have discovered that this is one of the simplest and most effective ways to slow me down and keep me connected with the presence of God throughout my day. Even in moments when I am overwhelmed by fear or distracted by the noise of the world, I can speak out my breath prayer and reconnect with God's heart in the middle of whatever is going on. A breath prayer can be as simple as, "Jesus, I love you," or, "Here I am." One of my favorite rhythms of the breath prayer is from Brennan Manning when he encourages a simple process of sitting comfortably in silence, and as you inhale, quietly whispering the name "Abba" and as you exhale, softly saying, "I belong to you."[7] Although these prayers are just a few simple words, they can become moments of deep connection with God that will bring nourishing life to your heart and soul.

Prompt: Take a few moments to slow down and ask the Lord to help you choose a breath prayer that you will use for this next season of your life. Remember, it is only a few words that you can speak in one breath. After you have chosen a simple phrase, take some time to a pray these words a few times to the Lord. Then, as you go back into your normal day, remember you can pray these words at any point and commune with His presence in whatever is going on. May this prayer become a well-worn path leading you again and again to the heart of God and deepening your friendship with Him.

photograph by MELISSA HELSER

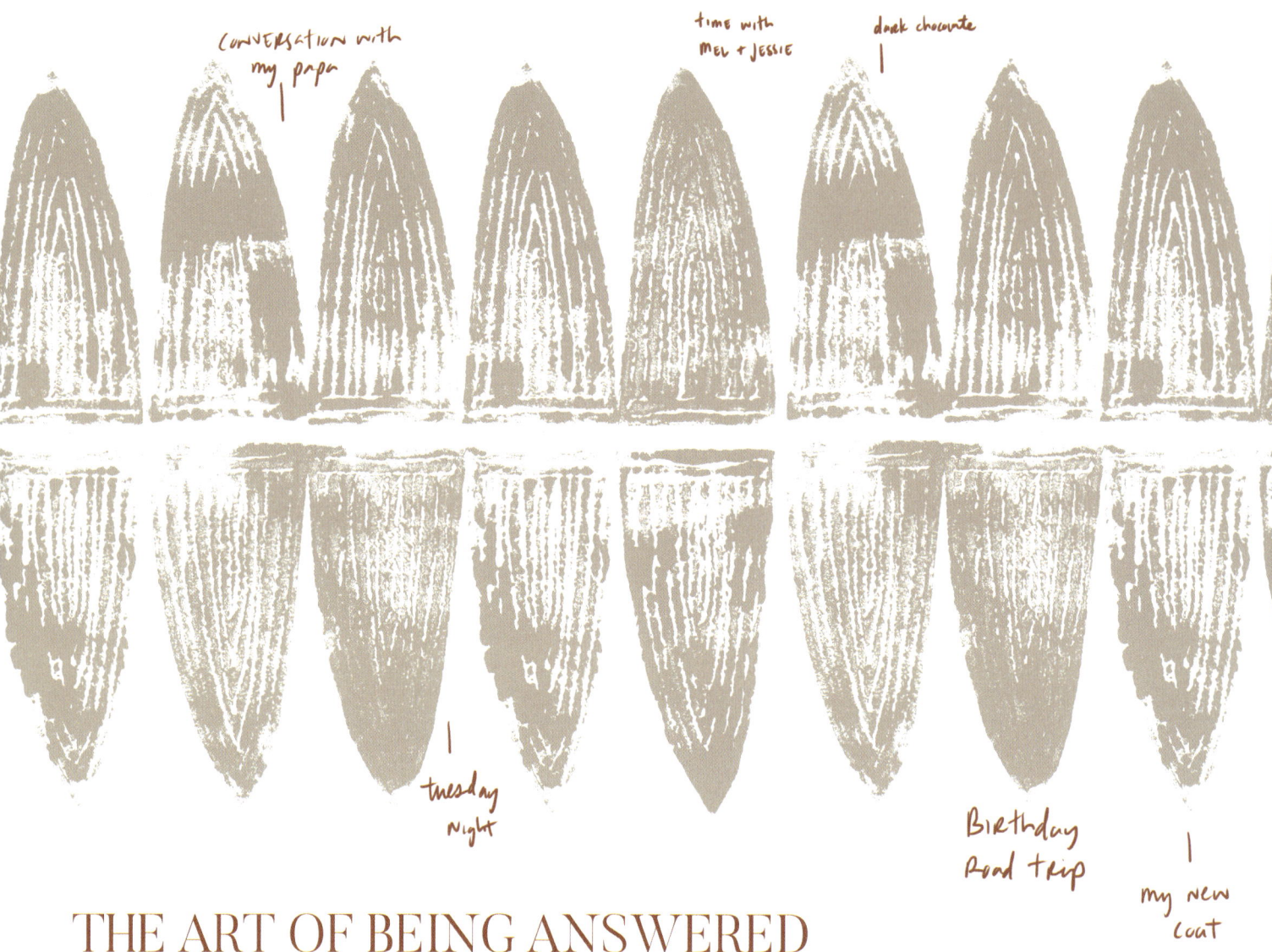

THE ART OF BEING ANSWERED

History Book prompt and print by JUSTINA STEVENS

It is easy in our culture to become obsessed with what we want God to do in our relationships, finances and jobs—demanding things from Him, and once we get them, we think a mere "thanks" is enough. However, I think that God's gifts are meant to transform us and need to be reflected on. It's vital that we learn to look back on our lives and see how God answers our prayers, fulfills our desires and partners with us in our simple yet profound lives. God's goodness is too easy to overlook, and gratitude has become less of our cultural norm. One of the greatest weapons we have is our remembrance and thanksgiving.

When the Israelites were in the desert, one of the greatest attacks was against their memory. They forgot the kindness of God and how He delivered them from their enemies. They lost heart and lost remembrance. In my own life, it is really easy for me to focus on places where I want and desire to see growth, and never acknowledge the growth that is happening right under my nose.

Today, you have the opportunity to engage creativity and gratitude through mark-making and color-mixing. This is a simple rhythm that feels pressure-free and fun. I invite you to take a deep breath and let all this mark-making be a way of focusing your thoughts toward gratitude. This prompt isn't as much about making a pretty picture as it is about cultivating a life of remembrance and gratitude.

For context, a History Book is a huge part of our rhythms in our discipleship school, the 18 Inch Journey. It is a visual journal that centers around the power of remembrance and celebrating life with God through recording visuals instead of just words. You don't have to have a History Book to complete this prompt, you can use watercolor paper, or a mixed media journal.

1. To begin, you will want to reflect on something specific, like a special or simple day, a trip or an event like moving to a new home, or one of your children hitting a milestone. For the sake of this lesson, my example will be the month leading up to a special birthday.

2. Turn on one of your favorite songs and start doodling on a piece of paper. My definition of doodling is mindlessly drawing for enjoyment or relief.

3. Once the song ends, look over your doodles. Try to find one shape in your work that is interesting and simple. You should aim to find a shape that isn't iconic, so avoid a heart shape or a star shape, and go for

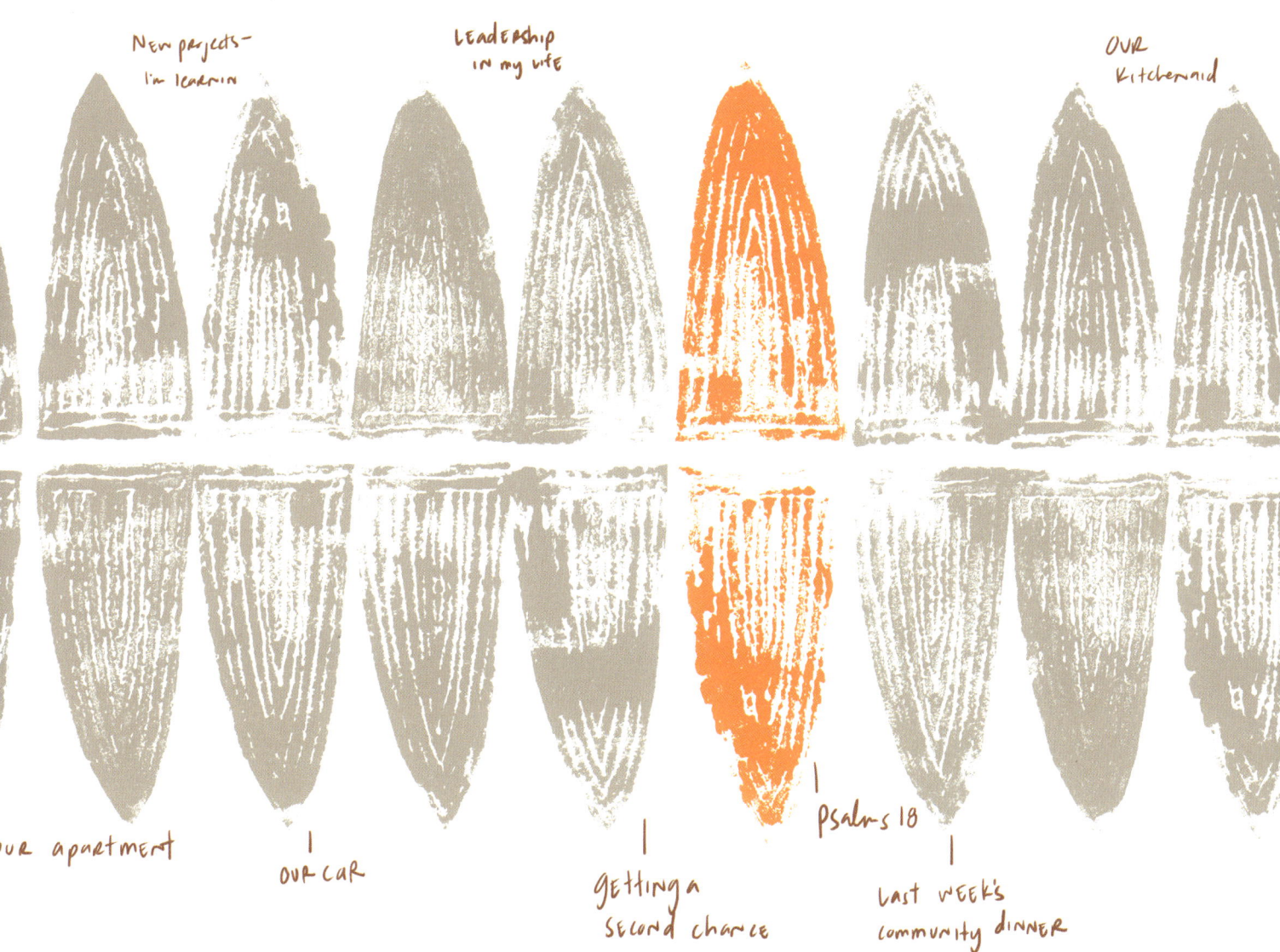

something a little less familiar. Like a swirl, or a triangle or an interesting line. Once you settle on the one you like, circle it on your doodle.

4. Then open up your journal or History Book to two clean pages—this is called a layout—and begin to draw the shape you chose from your doodle across the layout. Try your best to make these shapes connect, and draw at least ten across the pages.

5. As you draw, reflect on the Father's heart toward you. Meditate on moments that you have felt answered by Him through this specific season or event in time. Where in your life are you witnessing breakthrough, peace, joy, help and delight from your Heavenly Father? Can you see Him through the kindness of a friend's eye contact? Can you see Him in that job promotion? Or in your child's growth and laughter? Push yourself to start seeing the goodness of God in your simple life.

6. Choose a color scheme of two to three colors. Color schemes are such a powerful tool when creating visual art and it is important that you choose colors that you enjoy but aren't visually overwhelming and distracting. Once you've settled on a color palette, begin to fill in your shapes with the colors in a way that is interesting to you. These colors can even reflect the specific event you're focusing on. For my event, it was when the flowers were in bloom and color was emerging after a very cold winter. Therefore, my color palette reflects the burst of color I was seeing all around me. Granted, I still stuck to two to three colors so that my composition wasn't overwhelming.

7. Once you are done painting, label each shape as a representation of the places you have been answered and met by God. Allow your heart to fall into thankfulness as you list and record the answers and goodness of the Father. Turn your pattern into a diagram of sorts, revealing a written list of places you feel answered. You can write inside the shapes, beside the shapes or make a list next to what you've drawn. As you label each shape, I want to challenge you to find really simple and really deep moments. In my example, I saw the kindness of God in chocolate. Now, it's silly, but at the same time I have to become a person who can experience God through my senses and acknowledge that He does care about me encountering His love through what I enjoy. A deep moment in my example would be a conversation I had with my grandfather. He and I exchanged some profound stories; it is a conversation I will treasure my whole life. Title your page, "The Art of Being Answered," and include the date. Then step back and reread what you wrote. Feel connected to God through thanksgiving and let yourself feel proud of the work of your hands!

SAVOR

writing by MELISSA HELSER
photography from Melissa's
personal collection 2013

:to delight in, enjoy or
appreciate completely.

I bought her the shoes...tough and strong, made for the woods and walking. Waterproof, for puddles and the creek. The kind of shoes that you can get caught in a sudden downpour of liquid love from Heaven in with no worries. Every country girl needs adventure shoes. Shoes that can take you somewhere. I bought her a beautiful wool sweater; gloriously thick and meant for staying warm and feeling safe. Good quality, so she could wear it, trash it, wash it and put on its warmth again and again. This is not a special occasion sweater, but an everyday sweater. A sweater to enjoy the woods in the winter.

Our last name is Helser which means *people of the woods*; a fitting name for a family that treasures the woods in every season. They are a part of our every day, and today was an invitation to more. She insisted on packing a snack for the walk. That's when I knew it was going to be a long one. "We always take a snack," she informed me. Today it was going to be hot chocolate, giant marshmallows and crisp gala apples. The best of both worlds. Haven loves simple things. She is delightful in every way, even in something as simple as packing a snack. She stuffed it in the backpack and we were off. The long walks she usually takes just with Dad, but on this day I decided to tag along. I wanted to catch a glimpse of the glory of the deep woods in the barren winter and the deep love between a father and daughter. Their love is something to behold. It is like they understand each other in a way that I can't truly describe. I take it in carefully. I try to savor.

Savoring is an art that humans have long forgotten, but something we are craving to restore. Turn off the noise, lay down the chaos and maybe just take a long walk. Walk for beauty's sake, walk for relationship's sake; walk for no reason at all, and usually your soul finds a reason before you're done. I had forgotten that our woods in the winter are full of magic and wonder. I had forgotten that the trees speak loud in the quiet of their bareness. I had forgotten that the Holy Spirit speaks loud in the silence of winter. He said to me as I walked and observed the beauty, "Melissa, savor the clarity that the winter brings. In her bareness she shows you all her secrets, and in the spring she will clothe herself again—covering up her deep beauty." Sometimes I understand what He says, and sometimes I smile and know that I will understand as I mature in life; but today I knew exactly what He meant. I could see so far because of the bareness. I could see the contour of the land, the way the hills rise and fall and the way the trees cover her floor like a rolling chorus of melody and strength. Clarity in the winter. They're alive, not dead. They are sleeping but still speaking. The winter is beautiful. I receive.

We walked to their favorite place: the creek. It sometimes flows with rushing glory and other times trickles with quiet reverence. Today it was full to the brim and moving with power. This is the land my love grew up on, and this is the creek his daddy took him to. A tradition that has woven itself into the tapestry of our family. Traditions are beautiful when

rooted in love. They create a safe place of intentionality for those who choose to partake. I love that my love brought me to his home to live a simple, beautiful life. He is the kind of father that takes time to do the things that really matter in our children's hearts. The things that are the building blocks of the way they love and see life. I observed them walking hand in hand, singing together hand in hand, talking hand in hand and in the watching, I fell in love with him more and more. We walked along the edge of the creek for a long time before she found the perfect spot to stop and sit and savor. Deeper and deeper into the woods we went until she smiled, and I immediately knew we were there.

Backpack off, she drops to her knees. Opening the thermos of steaming hot chocolate, she is delighted. You see, Haven loves chocolate and always has. She loves it, and any chance she gets to have it, no matter what the form, fills her heart with pure joy. Today was no exception. Haven loves beauty and even with something as simple as a snack, she wanted to prepare it and make it beautiful. Giant, white, marshmallows plop into the tiny cups...another smile of affirmation fills her face. She looks at me, "Savor." That is all she says.

Such a simple word causes the heart to slow down and take delight in a moment. It provokes the soul to stop and breathe a little slower. It opens the eyes to see, truly see. I stop, I look, I listen. I watch a daughter being delighted in, and a father delighting. I listen to the laughter and join in the chorus. I savor the beauty of love and joy and realize that I am in a holy moment; an eternal moment. A moment I will never have again. I stop and see the burning bush of His presence. I take off my shoes...I breathe it in, and in the breathing I am changed. Changed by love. Changed by delight. By delighting, I feel delighted in. I am full. I marvel at the power of moments. Once again I am changed by something simple. Something seemingly meaningless, but to her, to him, to me, it is life and life abundant.

Prayer: "Father, give me eyes to see the glory of the moments you are living in. Teach me to slow down and breathe you in. I ask for a new perspective on life and love and joy. I ask for a newness in my heart to really live life and enjoy the privilege of the air in my lungs and life in my soul. You are the Giver of Life and I thank you in this moment for giving me the gift of life. I ask, God, that you help me to not waste it with empty busyness and clutter of the soul. Come in my heart and make space. Space for stillness. Space for joy. Space for laughter. Space for life. I receive the remodeling of my inner space...make room Holy Spirit, room for you. Show me the beauty of the seasons and help me to see, truly see."

RECIPE FOR RECEIVING THE LOVE OF GOD

"Every single moment you are thinking of me! How precious and wonderful to consider that you cherish me constantly in your every thought! O God, your desires toward me are more than the grains of sand on every shore! When I awake each morning, you're still with me" (Psalm 139:17-18, TPT).

How can we love God until we've received His love first? The Bible says that we love Him because He first loved us (see I John 4:19), but how often do we stop to allow the Father to love us or acknowledge the love He is giving us?

God's thoughts toward us are more numerous than the sand on every shore. If this is true, then we don't need to beg God to speak to us. Instead, we need to tune into the unending, infinite number of His thoughts for us—thoughts that are always encouraging and life-giving. Just like a radio doesn't need to write the songs it broadcasts, we don't need to make up what God is thinking of us; we just need to tune into the song He is singing.

One way that I've received God's love and thoughts over my life is through love songs. I remember a specific season of my life when Bon Iver's cover of "Can't Make You Love Me" by Bonnie Raitt was on repeat. If you've never heard it, it is a haunting song full of longing and vulnerability. The vocals dancing on the backdrop of playful piano keys brought the reality of God's love for me to light in a new way.

GRAINS of SAND

Every time I hear that song, I feel wooed by the Lord again. I am so moved by His willingness to pursue me with no guarantee that I will respond. He will love me whether I love Him or not. This extravagance moves my heart and I must respond. How can I not give Him my heart when His is bleeding for me? How can I not give Him my whole life when He comes to the deepest parts of my humanity, vulnerable and willing to feel pain.

Our God is willing to feel the heartache of rejection in His pursuit of us. He is not standing safely on the sidelines or playing it cool behind His wealth and power. No, He is willing to let us break His heart by honoring our power to choose Him. He is not a cookie-cutter lover that controls the outcome. My heart is won by His willingness to get messy and risk pain. And His love songs for us speak to both the beauty and anguish of love.

Prompt: For this recipe, we're going to give God the opportunity to cherish us through His thoughts in a love song. You will need one of your favorite love songs (just one!) and your journal. Play your song and listen to it. Are there certain words and phrases that you feel are capturing the Father's love for you? Let Love lavish your heart with His thoughts for you. He is patient, kind and does not fail. Ask the Father what He is singing to you through this song. Take some time to listen to His voice. Then write down what you hear Him saying to you.

by JD GRAVITT

OPENING UP

"For God is greater than our worried hearts and knows more about us than we do ourselves." I John 3:20, MSG

Sometimes the hardest thing to do is open up. To let God really see you, to admit when you feel like a mess, is so vulnerable. All the shame, all the questions—they can feel like chains, keeping you tight. You try to move to the Light, but Shame whispers, "He won't want you like this." You might push through and begin to feel the Light's sweet warmth of hope, but then it comes again, "You fraud, how dare you move on." Sometimes you may not even be sure why you feel ashamed. You're not exactly sure what you did wrong, but you still *feel* wrong. When you think of being vulnerable and honest with God, there is a tightness in your chest that holds you back. *There must be something wrong with me.* You take the bait. You believe it. You punish yourself, fearing that you deserve it. You hide from God in the corners of your heart. You resist, afraid to expose yourself to the only One who can heal your worried heart.

Friend, you are not too much. Your darkness is not dark to Him. He knows what you know. He understands your struggle and all this hiding is only causing more pain. You need the Light and His voice. You have seen much, but He has seen all. Remember, He is kind and patient. He will come to where you are. He will wrap His wings of deliverance around you and keep you warm. He is present—beside you even now as you read. The chains, the shame and the fear that He is not who He says He is *(at least not for you)* are all a trick. He will always offer you closeness. As you open up in trust, the Light of Jesus will swallow your fear and your peace will return. You are the one He longs for. You always have been and nothing can change that.

by JESSIE MILLER

FINDING HOME

RECIPE FOR FINDING HOME IN GOD

writing and art by JUSTINA STEVENS

From the ages of nineteen to twenty-four, I moved around a lot. In fact, I lived in ten different homes, apartments and dorms, constantly tugging along my car full of belongings. Logically, it seems like I would have begun to shed belongings after a while, but instead I ended up collecting more. I'd visit my parents and cram a few more things in their attic, I'd store things in friends' houses and lend things out part-time. A promise to one day pick up such-and-such thing in a year or so.

In the beginning, moving was exciting, but the constant change led me to wonder, *Do I have a home? Do I even know what home is?* Parts of my heart were in the mountains and on the coast, in the city and in the country. I was in love with busyness, broken and longing for the quiet, obsessed with "making it" and keeping most people at a distance. I experienced so much loss and tragedy in that cluster of years. All I knew to do was to keep moving, and ignore the questions in my heart. With every new pack-up and move-in, the longing for home heightened and revealed something deeper in my heart. *Did I know my home—my real home in Jesus?* The exhaustion from life and moving was real, but the great ache that was in my heart was for settling with the Trinity. I wanted the courage to slow down.

When I graduated college and moved into community, it took me much longer than I wanted to settle down. Once my feet stopped running, I found my mind was the hardest thing to quiet. I had to collect myself from so much responsibility, from so many places, and put all the pieces before God. Though painful, now I know that in God's kindness He gave me the privilege of unraveling. In His kindness, He showed me every untrue thing I had believed about Him and exchanged His love for my tattered opinions. As I gave up control and let the Father heal me, I found the deepest desire for home answered.

I have learned that healing and transforming require listening to truth every day. Leaning into the voice of the Lord even when I don't feel like it, even when it sounds like the exact opposite of my circumstance, even when it seems pointless, is worth it. Because the truth is, my submission to Jesus does gather up a sudden shift in my life. There were seasons when that submission gathered and gathered and gathered for years and suddenly, my heart was different. One of the greatest realizations of my life was that God enjoyed putting me back together. The Trinity is a family that loves to adopt and mend, there is no way around it. I am confident that it is one of their greatest joys.

One way that I practice submission to Jesus is through reading the Bible. This may be an old school idea for some of you, but hear me out. I choose a chapter of the Bible every year and focus on it. I decide not to abandon it even if it gets boring or falls flat. I sit with it every day and let it transform me. Then I write a responsive prayer to God to pray all through my day in certain seasons. I take the most impactful language and meditate on it, and then own the places where I deeply struggle with the truth of the Scripture and repent. I love repenting throughout the day. It's been a game changer for me.

Here is the chapter I meditated on and my responsive prayer from that season in my mid-twenties when I needed God to mend me:

"But me he caught—reached all the way from sky to sea; he pulled me out of that ocean of hate, that enemy chaos, the void in which I was drowning. They hit me when I was down, but God stuck by me. He stood me up on a wide-open field; I stood there saved—surprised to be loved! God made my life complete when I placed all the pieces before him. When I got my act together, he gave me a fresh start. Now I'm alert to God's ways; I don't take God for granted. Every day I review the ways he works; I try not to miss a trick. I feel put back together, and I'm watching my step. God rewrote the text of my life when I opened the book of my heart to his eyes." Psalm 18:16-24, MSG

My prayer: "God, I soften my heart before you. I remember that you made me, and know me better than I know myself. I open my hands and let you see every piece of my life. You are the giver of fresh starts, I stand in this truth. I repent for believing that you are too busy and careless to mend me. I humble my heart and ask for a new perspective, remind me of the home I have in you. I invite you to speak to me."

Prompt: Take a moment with the Psalm above and let it impact you. Then, pray my prayer, and write God's response to you. Step out in faith to record His truth over your life! In any season, you can meditate on a specific Scripture and write a responsive prayer. I encourage you to give it a try. You can tape up your Scripture and prayer on the wall or window where you wash dishes, or on your bathroom mirror. This is a great way to practice making room for Jesus throughout your day. In the simple acts of cleaning or preparing for the day, you can engage His truth.

LISTEN AGAIN

A RECIPE FOR ENJOYING SCRIPTURE

by ALLIE SAMPSON / *photograph by* MORGAN CAMPBELL

"Leaving that place, Jesus withdrew to the region of Tyre and Sidon. A Canaanite woman from that vicinity came to him, crying out, 'Lord, Son of David, have mercy on me! My daughter is demon-possessed and suffering terribly.' Jesus did not answer a word. So his disciples came to him and urged him, 'Send her away, for she keeps crying out after us.' He answered, 'I was sent only to the lost sheep of Israel.' The woman came and knelt before him. 'Lord, help me!' she said. He replied, 'It is not right to take the children's bread and toss it to the dogs.' 'Yes it is, Lord,' she said. 'Even the dogs eat the crumbs that fall from their master's table.' Then Jesus said to her, 'Woman, you have great faith! Your request is granted.' And her daughter was healed at that moment" (Matthew 15:21-28, NIV).

It was a passage I'd read many times before. Sitting with a group of friends during one of our annual discipleship schools, we were reading through the Gospels and were quickly approaching Matthew 15. I could feel myself tensing up as it inevitably came closer. I'd read it countless times, and every time I did, I'd skim over it as quickly as possible. To be honest, it made me squirm a little. When I read it, Jesus sounded unnecessarily harsh and void of compassion. I couldn't reconcile the severity of His words with the nature I knew Him to have.

I couldn't wrap my mind around it, much less my heart. I felt the all-too-familiar cringe and confusion coil around me. And then—a still, small voice. "Allie, do I have permission to show you something new?"

"Yes, Lord," I replied, practicing humbling my heart. I closed my eyes and took a deep breath. I reminded myself: *God is mysterious. He is not a riddle to be solved but a Father to be connected with.* Opening my eyes, I read the challenging words again.

As I finished reading the passage, I felt the Holy Spirit draw near and offer me a chance to practice honesty: "Allie, what do you hear me saying to this woman?"

"I don't know, Lord. It sounds harsh. Severe. It sounds like you're belittling her." His reply came kindly, "My daughter, read it again. Try to hear the tone in my voice. What if I wasn't diminishing her? What if I was repeating back to her what the world had taught her to believe?"

As I read the words again, something changed. Instead of Jesus reprimanding this woman with cultural sneers, I heard a different tone in His voice. It was like I could see the scene play out in front of me: Jesus stopping, listening. Desperate tears running down her face. And when she works up the courage to ask for what she needs, Jesus repeats back to her the disqualification she would have heard her whole life. In this moment, reading this passage, instead of hearing condemnation and diminishment, I heard Jesus creating an opportunity for this woman's faith to rise up.

I saw Him hold up a metaphorical mirror to her face and give her the chance to see herself. It was another "Who do you say I am?" moment, much like Jesus had with Peter. There, in front of the disciples, Jesus looked this woman in the eyes and repeated back to her everything that the world would have taught her to expect from Him.

I was overwhelmed with emotion as I imagined her despair turning into relief. And in the way that only Jesus can, I felt the miracle taking place in my own heart—my own despair and desperation to know Jesus blooming into relief with the understanding that Jesus is better than I believe Him to be. He was willing to make an exception for this woman, to break the rules for her. And in that moment I knew, He was willing to break the rules for me, too.

Now, I am no Bible scholar. And I don't believe that this is the one and only way to interpret this passage. But I do know that in that moment, Jesus came and revealed Himself to me. I also know it changed my life forever. Instead of shying away from difficult Scripture, this interaction with Him helped me understand this truth: that in order to understand Scripture, I have to humble my heart and ask the Spirit who inspired it to come and teach me what it means.

Since then, I've had countless moments where I feel the Father come and correct the way I'm perceiving His tone. In times of reading my Bible, in times of journaling His voice, I've felt Him draw close and say, "Allie, you're reading my words as if I'm an angry parent. Read them again, and this time, remember that I discipline the ones I love. Find the compassion and kindness in my voice." Each time I practice posturing my heart in the truth that I am irrefutably loved by Him, I can more accurately hear His tone. This is our very loving, kind Father we are talking about. Even in correction, even in hard truth, He is true to His nature: "The Lord is compassionate and merciful, slow to get angry and filled with unfailing love" (Psalm 103:8, NLT).

I have found that hearing God's tone often requires me to first take the time to remember His nature, and second, to call myself to wake up out of the slumber of familiarity. When I become too familiar with a story in the Bible, it's easy for me to assume I already know exactly how it unfolded. In this posture, there is no room for mystery. My assumptions retell the same story, and I walk away feeling either bored or full of religious pride. What a tragic way to commune with the Word Who Became Flesh! I was made for a more fulfilling communion than this. And friend, so were you.

Just like properly understanding a written message from someone—be it a text message, an email, a letter—requires knowing that person's intention and tone, I must ask the Holy Spirit to help me understand when I read the voice of the Lord. To misinterpret His tone is to misinterpret His heart. May we become children who are courageous and humble enough to ask our Father to help us understand His nature.

Prompt: Take a deep breath and invite the Holy Spirit to come sit with you. Ask Him to bring to mind a time when you misinterpreted the tone in His voice. Perhaps it's a passage of Scripture that tends to rub you the wrong way. Maybe it's a time you journaled His voice and you heard it through a filter of diminishment or condemnation. Practice humbling your heart and invite the Lord to reveal Himself to you by praying this prayer: "Jesus, I long to know you. Please forgive me for misinterpreting your heart. Holy Spirit, help me to hear Jesus' voice, just as He promised in John 10:27. Take me back to His words and help me hear His tone rightly. I welcome you to change my mind. Amen."

TRUSTING HIS NATURE

Consider this: you go out to your mailbox and discover that three of your best friends have invited you to an incredible party. How would you normally respond to that letter?

by MOLLY SKAGGS
block prints by MORGAN CAMPBELL

If they are three of your most beloved friends, I would hope that you would jump for joy and excitement over being invited to spend time celebrating life with them. It would be silly for you to sit back in suspicion, doubting their love for you in that moment, don't you think? Rather than question their goodness and their intentions, you would call them up immediately and say, "Yes! Count me in. See you at the party!"

I would hope to do the same myself, yet I find that sometimes when I open up the Trinity's invitations to me, my first response is to doubt God and challenge His intentions toward me. It causes me to wonder: *Why would I have such a knee-jerk reaction to the Lord reaching out to me like that?* I have been learning how this kind of response really has nothing to do with what He's like; rather, it has more to do with how I am seeing God's friendship through my own broken perspective. What kind of a friend am I viewing God as? Unsafe. Untrustworthy. A friend who actually wants to deceive me into failure and humiliation rather than celebrate the gift of abundant life and closeness He so handsomely paid to give to me.

The good news is that I can take comfort in knowing that God fully understands how fearful I am to actually live and experience all the blessings He has for me. Out of all the friends we have, He is the most compassionate and understanding. He is Love! For me to believe that He

What would happen if we trusted His nature and started receiving His invitations to love, beauty and celebration?

could, even for one moment, be anything but trustworthy and safe is to indeed question His goodness—to indict His true nature and question the reality of whether He is 100% Goodness or not. Oh how sad I am when I discover, through Holy Spirit's help, that I actually believe this! So, what to do about it? The best way to get out of this cycle of distrust and doubt is to repent and turn back to the Lord. Being given the opportunity to repent is one of His greatest gifts to us! When I am caught again in a moment of fear giving way to unbelief, I can own that I was believing lies about His heart, ask Him for forgiveness, and break my agreement by yielding to and declaring the truth. It could look something like this: "Father, I want to humble my heart before you again. I own that I have believed lies about your heart and distrusted your nature. I have been questioning your intentions for me and doubting your goodness. I am so sorry. Will you forgive me? I want to be fully connected with you again. I yield my heart and cling to the truth that you are trustworthy, that you only have good things for me, and that in every invitation you offer, you are offering the best of yourself. I receive your love and say yes to your offer of deeper friendship. Lord, I trust you."

The Word tells us that it is God's kindness that leads us to repentance (see Romans 2:4). He means for life to be experienced and enjoyed to the fullest with Him. He is always so ready to forgive and help us receive His abundance. What would happen if we trusted His nature and started receiving His invitations to love, beauty and celebration? It would mean that our hearts are being perfected in Love and not hiding away for fear of punishment. We would have a whole new outlook on what life really is—an adventure and risk meant to be experienced in joy with God. It would mean that the eyes of our hearts have been touched and healed again. That we would see God for who He is and always will be: our dearest and most trustworthy friend who is longing to celebrate us and live out the risk of life with us.

PROMPT: Think back to a recent moment where God offered you an invitation to something that both delighted and frightened you (for example: a new promotion at your job, being asked on a date with someone new, the opportunity to connect with a respected leader or mentor, or being asked to share your opinion with a group). Ask the Lord, "Why was my reaction towards fear so strong in this?" Journal His response to you, allowing Him to speak love and clarity into your heart. End by writing out your own prayer of repentance, breaking agreement with fear and turning your heart back toward trusting His nature.

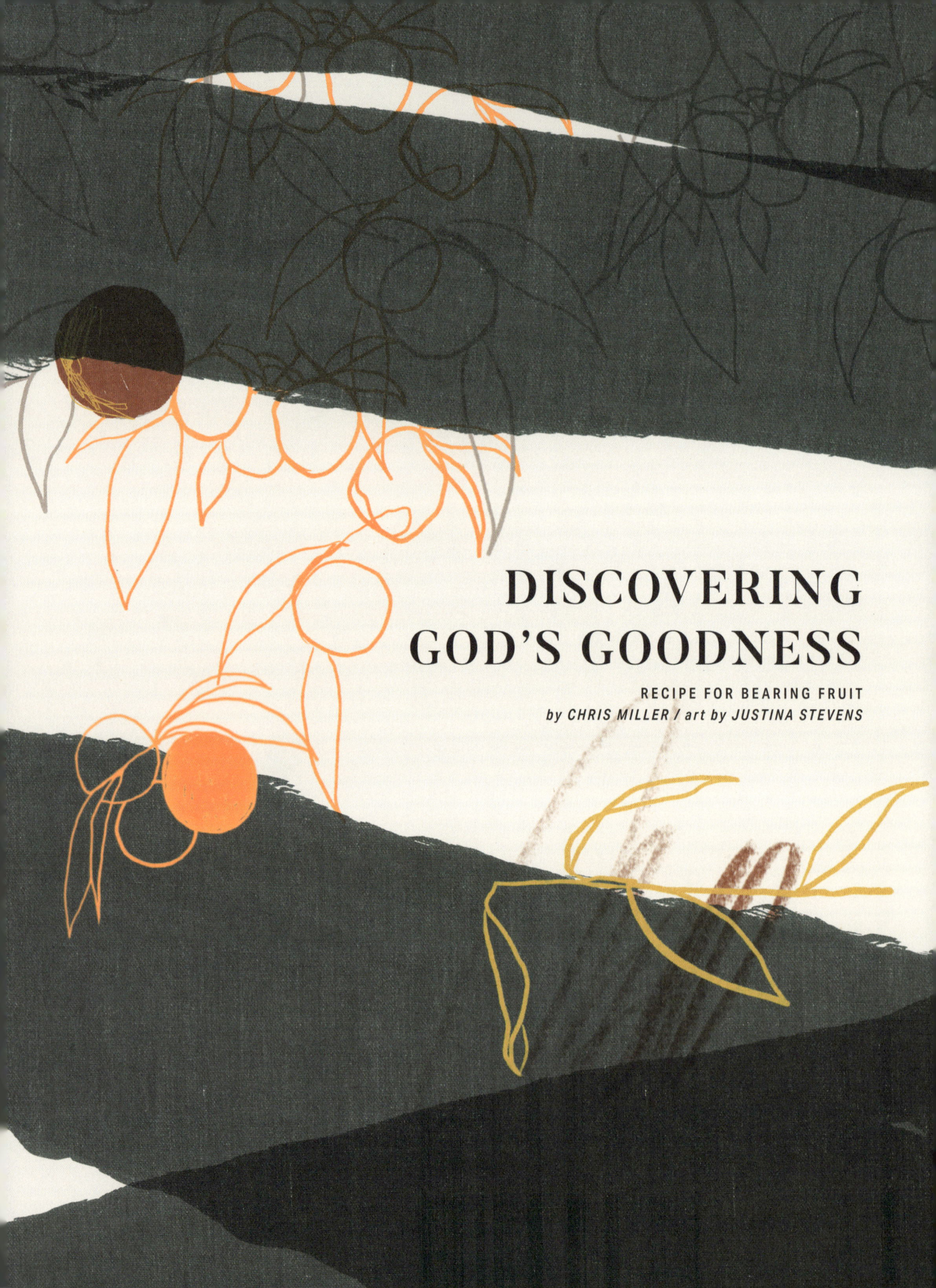

DISCOVERING GOD'S GOODNESS

RECIPE FOR BEARING FRUIT

by CHRIS MILLER / art by JUSTINA STEVENS

> "He is like a tree planted by streams of water, that yields its fruit in its season and its leaf does not wither. In all that he does, he prospers." Psalm 1:3, ESV

On a springtime trip to Florida, our community had the privilege of visiting a Valencia orange grove where thousands of acres of the fruit were grown and harvested for juicing. Lee, a brilliant farmer and an inspired inventor, led us through row after row of the best pesticide-free oranges in the state. Elated, we picked fresh oranges from the trees and used our pocket knives to cut into the top of the bright fruit, squeezing fresh juice into our thirsty mouths, letting it run down our faces under the scorching afternoon sun.

As we stumbled over ant hills with juice stained faces and sticky hands, our new friend explained that many young orange trees must be exhaustively pruned for the first few years of their lives to ensure maturity and to sustain long-term growth. Oftentimes, an orange tree sapling will focus all of its energy and nutrients on bearing fruit in a young state, before it has reached full maturity. In striving to produce fruit, the immature tree will starve itself of the nutrients it so desperately needs to develop. It will die long before its time. Lee, a wise farmer, knows that the anxious young tree must be pruned back until it has learned the way to yield. In love, he teaches the tree what it cannot teach itself. I propose that if we too are known and recognized by our fruit, then just like the orange tree, we must yield ourselves to our heavenly Father to be pruned so that we may mature, sustain long-term growth and produce true fruit. This is an invitation to growth unlike anything we have ever known.

Our Father, being the great gardener that He is, must prune and cut away that which is not life-giving so that we can be whole, lacking nothing. In the pain that accompanies true growth, we may not perceive the pruning process to be good. Only a good gardener would risk a fruitless season to prepare the tree for a lifetime of fruit. When we abide in His perfect love and trust His vision, we will be the trees that bear beautiful fruit and give glory to Him continuously.

Prompt: I want to challenge you to read the following prayer and then craft your own prayer to the Father in your journal. Be honest with God and get real with your heart. He wants your honesty!

"Father, I repent for believing the lie that you are not good, and for questioning your motives as you come to prune and cleanse my heart. I confess that you alone are the source of life and that your plans for me are perfect. I invite your Holy Spirit into the garden of my heart to prune everything that is keeping me from the fullness you have for me. I believe that you have my best in mind, and I trust your vision for my life."

Now, quiet your heart and invite the Holy Spirit. Ask the Father, "What are your intentions in pruning my heart? What fruit are you growing in me this season?" Let Him speak to you and then journal what you hear Him saying.

THE BENCH

RECIPE FOR SAFETY WITH GOD
by MARY HALL / *photograph by* PHYLLIS UNKEFER

"Yahweh is my best friend and shepherd. I always have more than enough. He offers a resting place for me in his luxurious love…" Psalm 23:1-2, TPT

My mother's side of the family is Gullah. We are African-American people who live in the Lowcountry regions and sea islands primarily in South Carolina and Georgia. We have a distinct culture of language, food and heritage that has flourished and been preserved since the times of slavery. Mount Pleasant, South Carolina is where my Nana always had pots boiling on the stove for any passerby or neighbor who would come around for one of "Miss Maggie's plates," where my uncle would fix bikes in the yard, where the radio was playing loud and the laughter from my aunties would echo even louder in my heart. In the middle of our family reunions, Thanksgiving holidays and more, I would find a time to sneak away and go on a bike ride by myself—smelling the sea air, cruising down the street barefoot in a dress. Each time, I would go to a bench down a quiet, hidden street that faces the water. It always soothed me to go there as a girl—to sit in the stillness and stare at the water. I felt my true self there, in a land by the water that my people have called home for generations. I felt beautiful, at home and safe.

Last year, when I was spending time with the Lord, I asked Him for a picture of where He wanted to meet me when I felt overwhelmed. He reminded me of this memory and took me to that bench by the coast. I saw Him there sitting next to me, bikes laying on the ground. Just looking at the ocean. Quiet. Still. Seagulls floating by. He just wanted to be there with me. He liked having me close. And in that picture, He called me beloved and I believed Him. I knew that I was safe and that my identity was secure in Him. He didn't want anything except the pleasure of being with me.

God is a speaking God who loves to engage us through our imaginations. I am grateful that when the Lord formed and knit humans together, He put an imagination in all of us with the intention for it to be a place of connection and creativity with Him. In the forefront of my thoughts and mind, there He is creating life, waiting for me to call, promising that He will answer and speak to me. In the recesses of my imagination and perception, He is there, smiling, flipping over tables, clearing out clutter and whispering sweet nothings (which are actually sweet everythings) to me. He is always available.

In my continual journey of reclaiming myself as the beloved of God, this became a sacred picture that I returned to for months. If I got overwhelmed by work projects in the middle of the day, He would whisper, "Mary, the bench." I would imagine myself there and be flooded with the realization that He is with me. Before I would go up on a stage to speak to people, I'd feel a hand on my shoulder, "The bench." I would center back on God and His approval and confidence in me as I took the stage. And even now, in hard moments when I get triggered, where do I go? The bench.

This has been a sacred practice for me. Going to this place of safety with the Lord in my imagination has given me a place to meet Him quickly in the middle of real, everyday life. When the accuser wants to tempt me to believe that I am an unworthy person, I go to the bench and remember and believe that Jesus is unashamed of me and calls me beloved.

Depending on the season, the Lord meets me in new and changing ways. At times, He'll be sitting across from me, we'll go somewhere new or He'll say something different to me. But, what doesn't change is that fact that He always offers me a resting place in His love to root myself in.

Prompt: Ask the Lord, "Will you give me a picture of our resting place in this season? What are you saying to me in this place?" Wait on Him. He wants to meet you in your imagination. It could be a place you have been before, or a place you've never been. What matters is that you feel connected and safe with Him. Moving forward, practice returning to this picture in the middle of your days, when you long to feel His nearness and safety.

UNLOCKING GRIEF

RECIPE FOR GRIEVING WITH GOD

by JAKE STEVENS / *art by* JUSTINA STEVENS

One day, the staff at our ministry was having a meeting after a long season of discipleship. It had been a tougher season for me. I had to overcome a lot more than I expected and I felt empty. Melissa looked around the room at all of us. We were visibly tired, but ready to thank God. She asked, "When was one moment that you knew God was smiling at you in this last season?" The room got quiet. I closed my eyes and asked the Lord to help me, because I wasn't sure. I've felt the pride of God over my life for sure, but connecting that to a smile was a new kind of challenge for me. After a few a minutes, a clear moment came to mind: I was spending time with a student in the wood shop, not really talking about much, when all of a sudden, our conversation turned into an opportunity for grief. He had lost his dad in his early twenties, a pain I understood very well having lost my own father when I was ten. This student opened his heart and we wept together.

When I opened my eyes in our meeting, Melissa asked me to share. As I explained the moment, I was gripped with empathetic sorrow for this student's story and the sacredness that my own story created a safe place for him to engage vulnerability. All the while, I was realizing God's smile over me because my loss didn't lead to bitterness and resentment. All those years of letting God into my grieving became a bridge for someone else to feel seen and understood.

A decade ago, grief didn't even feel like an option. Grief wasn't something that was modeled for me. And in my youth, years after my father passed, I didn't even realize that loss on that kind of level could be why I was in so much pain. It also seemed simpler to find things to numb the ache in my soul than to address it. Knowing what I know now, I believe grief shouldn't be done alone. I can recall the first time Jesus initiated grieving with me. It was through a leader wrapping their arms around me and letting me cry when I was nineteen. I can honestly say that that was one of the most profound encounters with the love of God I'd had until then. Love was holding hands with grief, and it was good.

It has been many years since my earthly father passed away from cancer. I've lived longer without him than with him. I can't deny that even now there is an ache in my heart. An ache for what could have been; a wondering, a wishing to have an "old guy" in my life to call on the phone for advice. But it is in this ache that God has come time and time again to help me accept my story, through shedding another layer of pain by grieving with Him and receiving a different gift. Gifts like: the group of amazing friends who are men of God in my life, getting to ask men who are further ahead of me in life for help, receiving the gift of the handyman I've made friends with. God has extended to me un-isolated fathering. I have been given many "fathers" in the loss of one father. I couldn't have received any of this without acknowledging that my pain is important, and is worth tending to by letting God into it and grieving with Him.

That moment in the wood shop was the first time this student had ever grieved the loss of his father with someone else. It was an unlocking grief moment. I know that the empathy I carry for the pain of loss helped remove loneliness and the barrier to his tears. Jesus lived by the example of giving and sharing with others, not keeping what He received just for Himself. The smile from God I felt in that meeting came, I believe, because I shared my healing with another and didn't hoard it for myself for fear of losing it. The fruit of me choosing to grieve with God is that it has helped others do the same. Fruit bears seeds and seeds bear more fruit trees.

Prompt: God can come and fill up the space of your greatest loss and transform it into a sacred space. Take out your journal, sit in the silence and ask the Father, "Is there a place of great pain in my story that you want to transform?" Journal His voice.

THE BIRCH

Somewhere in-between
The dammed up creek and the field of green
Is the uncharted land of cedar trees
Where the strong and solid grow

Brave souls this wood have pioneered
The trails they've blazed, the paths they've cleared
Have made space for these trees to thrive
And guide others along their way

Among the cedar it may seem odd to find
A Virginia Redwood and a Carolina Pine
But rooted firmly and deeply, side by side
These two have found depth of friendship

The Spruce, the Dogwood and the European Beech
Have found the sky within their reach
Their Winter's passed and their Spring arrived
The Life within them has emerged

But of all the trees tucked in this wood
I've both best and least understood
The birch that grows in rapid spurts
And then pushes her layers forward

At first I thought her rather strange
Was she lost, confused, angry, deranged?
Would it not be better for her to arrange
Herself to be more consistent?

I found myself looking with critical eyes
They misled me and I began to despise
This tree that would never realize
Her potential to be firm

I saw the cedars and began to compare
This birch to them and my temper flared
And I told the tree with a scolding glare
That she needed to be stronger

I encouraged her to harden her bark
To hide her lines that look so dark
And hoard her layers. So she became stark
And in Spring she still looked dead

It was then that I began to see
That the value crafted within this tree
Was too great and I had to set her free
From the pressure to be something she wasn't

"Wake up!" I said, "The season's right!
Unfurl your branches toward the Light
You're free to be whomever you like
Just teach me who you are."

Life shot up inside her veins
And in the midst of heavy April rain
She no longer mistook her peeling bark for pain
Green started to appear

Now this birch has been taught how to bend
To be flexible in raging wind
And with every season her branches extend
Higher than before

From this land this birch has come to learn
To not be so fickle or so stern
But that the consistency for which her heart so yearns
Looks a lot like weathered wood

by ALLIE SAMPSON

Does the Ocean Sleep Alone?

by JESSIE MILLER
photograph by MELISSA HELSER

When all is quiet on the dark glinting pallet,
Can the Sea hear her song?

Does she know what she sounds like
when all who move her are gone?

Unaffected yet connected,
All that move her still exist.
They swirl inside her, but on the surface,
Sleep.
She moves, her sound is soft.
She catches and cradles herself again and again.

And then God asks her,
What makes you beautiful, Sea? Them or me?
When are you, You? Then or now?
What is your song? Harmony or melody?

I do not know. Dare I say, I do not know?

I love the way I sound when birds are far from me.
I love the way my surface feels,
absent from sun's heat. I crave the time when
travelers choose a route other than me.

But Whale, he knows what's underneath.
And Sand, she knows me deep.
When Boat splits through my watery soul,
I feel I have achieved.

The things that rob my quiet song
are to whom I love to sing.

Forgive me, God.

She overflows.
He wraps the lovely Sea within
His arms she'll always be
and alone she'll never sleep.

a feature on

KEN HELSER

The Founder of A Place for the Heart

by ELLA ROSELT
photography by MELISSA HELSER

I am fascinated by hands—they're always one of the first things I notice about someone. I love how, in essence, my five fingers match your five fingers; and yet no two hands are exactly alike. The hands of someone who has worked hard, loved deeply, sacrificed greatly and lived life fully are the most fascinating. Our stories are written by our hands; on our hands. I love watching deft hands at work—hands that are skilled and sure with much experience. Hands that bear a callus here from the garden spade, a scar there from a carving tool. Hands that are strong on a fallen tree trunk, that lie gentle with blessing on a child's head. How beautiful are the feet of those who bring the good news and establish peace; how beautiful are the hands of those who work to sustain it (see Isaiah 52).

I have seen Papa Ken's hands on tractors, spades, hoes, all manner of garden implements. Thick with dirt, gingerly holding tiny seeds and seedlings. I have seen his fingers glide over piano keys, summoning melodies from its depths and praise from the depths of me. I have seen those same hands work with infinite patience and a paintbrush to bring to life the most breathtaking of watercolors. I have seen the fruit of his hands in the typed content of an email inbox or the inside jacket of a gift of a book—words of love and affirmation and wisdom. Hands that have touched and loved and worked and brought to life fifty-two acres of land in a place called Wisdom. Hands that have cherished and served a wife, children, grandchildren and countless others besides. And today these same hands are expertly, effortlessly working bread dough on a countertop. He smiles and his eyes almost disappear into crinkles, and joy overtakes his face. He tells me his story of bread. It begins with a young boy traveling with his daddy, delivering baking goods to the back doors of commercial kitchens. Catching the scent of baking bread, eating warm pieces handed to him, swallowing the love of both the process and its result. Next, the young man and his young bride entertaining his band at Christmas time on a young musician's budget—meeting guests at the door with steaming loaves of fresh-baked goodness, to slake hunger and enable the spaghetti meal to stretch further. Later, the older man and his family, the fruit of their lives impacting generations whilst the fruit of his hands fills bellies and awakens a deeper hunger of the heart. This is his story, and his story is still growing.

He has discovered that his hands do not need to be clasped in prayer in order that the Father may speak. In fact, Papa Ken knows that often when

his hands are busy, his ears are more attentive. While he's kneading dough, Jesus can show him where He's pressing on Ken's life. While he's trimming the grapevine, the Father shows him where He is doing His own work of pruning. As he says, "When I'm baking, I'm always in a place of worship. I've never made bread and the Lord didn't speak to me." The act of baking becomes a sacred act, and Papa Ken is quick to usher others into this holy place. The highlight of many a young person's summer has been time spent with Papa Ken, learning to bake bread: learning how to feel when the consistency of the bread dough is just right; and learning the feel of the Father's hands on their own lives.

Papa Ken prepares a biga in advance of his bread-baking: a simple mixture of flour, water and yeast that will add depth and richness of flavor to the bread, and help it to rise wonderfully. But when the actual making of the bread begins, the whole process takes only a couple of hours from start to finish. For hands that have toiled away at projects with the patience of years, or worked on paintings that have taken months, or crafted songs that have taken days, this simple process is a joy. The young man was a dreamer: his hands began many projects that he would never finish. He felt the invitation of the Father to question his own inability to follow through on so many things. He felt the joy of the Lord inside of him, the source and root of creativity, sparking to life all these projects and ideas. But it wasn't until the man was older that he understood that the joy of the Lord is not only the root of creativity, but the sustaining strength to finish what you start. The very woods of A Place for the Heart stand silent testimony to the fact that Papa Ken's hands know how to finish excellently what they have started joyfully. But the warm aroma of fresh-baked bread, and the delighted smiles of anticipation on the faces of his grandchildren, are a beautiful reward at the end of a simple task of service and love.

Papa Ken removes fresh loaves of bread from the oven, gently laying them out on a counter to cool. He places his now stilled hands on the counter, leaning his weight into them as he inhales deeply, "If someone's been baking bread and they invite you over, it doesn't really matter about the rest of the meal once you've caught the scent of that bread! The smell of bread will be enough to make the whole meal better. You know what I mean? There's a scripture that says that we're a sweet aroma to the Lord... Well, I think we should smell like fresh-baked bread!"

RECIPE FOR DEPENDENCY

BIG HANDS, TINY WINGS

by MOLLY KATE SKAGGS
art by JUSTINA STEVENS

"As a father has compassion on his children, so the Lord has compassion on those who fear him; for he knows how we are formed, he remembers that we are dust... from everlasting to everlasting the Lord's love is with those who fear him, and his righteousness with their children's children." Psalm 103:13-14,17, NIV

I was about eight years old when I had one of my most vivid encounters with kindness. My mom picked me up from school like any normal day. We pulled into our driveway, and as we reached our house, I looked out my window and saw what looked to be baby birds in the road. "Momma, look!" I cried out. She immediately slammed on the brakes to see what was wrong.

"Oh, honey," she said in a sad, pitying tone of voice, "those poor little birds must have fallen out of their nest while learning how to fly." Sure enough, there they were: three baby birds, frantically hopping and flapping their tiny wings, desperately trying to get away from us. There was no mother bird in sight. They were lost. They were so afraid, and I knew it, too. I could do nothing except cry my little heart out for them. Mom ran inside the house to get my dad to come help. Within moments, he was there next to me. "Daddy, can you help them?" I cried.

He crouched down beside me, gently pulling me closer to him. "I'll do my best, Sissy," he replied. Calmly and quietly, he approached the baby birds. Mom whispered careful remarks of being mindful that if he were to touch them, his scent would get all over them, and the mother might abandon them. My heart continued to break at that dreadful thought, but somehow I knew my dad could help the birds return to safety. I remember the stunning contrast of his bigness to their smallness. Without touching them, his compassionate hands carefully helped guide the birds onto the grass and out of the way. *Maybe now their mother will find them*, I thought. Yet what I remember most about that moment was the feeling that my dad could do anything; that this great big man I called Daddy was a hero. My hero. No matter how big or small things seemed, I knew that he would always be there, ready to save the day and restore the safety, trust and peace of my fragile little world. For surely if his heart had compassion on three helpless baby birds in need, how much more deeply did he love me and feel the pain of my breaking heart inside his own?

It is much the same way with our Heavenly Father—our Papa, who not only is bigger and stronger than us, but is the One whose heart is so tender towards all the things that ignite as well as break ours. He gets down low next to us, pulls us closer to Himself, and assures us with a warm tone how much He cares and that everything is going to be okay. Kindness is the very essence of the Father—every move He makes on our behalf is a direct offshoot from this place in His nature. It is what helps us to see our need for Him and what inspires us to turn back around and be changed by His love. We are all free birds and little children who fall out of the nest and have our hearts broken sometimes, even while learning how to fly. Who wants most to be there and help guide us to safety, as well as comfort our fearful sadness? Our incredibly good and kind Father does. Every time. And He longs to assure our hearts just how much He truly does care for us. He is our hero.

Prompt: Read Psalm 103:8-17. Take note of the verses that are gently pulling on your heart. In your journal, ask the Lord, "Father, what are you speaking about your kindness toward me today?" Journal His voice in response to you. Posture your heart to receive His kindness, for He cares so much for you and all that you care about.

THE PATIENT TEACHER

RECIPE FOR PATIENCE WITH YOURSELF

"Bear in mind that our Lord's patience means salvation." II Peter 3:15, NIV

When a violinist first begins to learn to play, there is an inevitable initial period during which they produce some of the most awful noises ever to penetrate the human ear. This is because it takes a while to learn a combination of skills: holding the violin and the bow correctly; drawing the bow over the strings at the right spot and with the right amount of firmness, but not too much; keeping the bow steady... What helps a student progress more quickly out of this ear-insulting phase is practice. Practice and patience. It doesn't happen overnight; it takes some long hours of dedicated work. If the students get frustrated with themselves, they may be stuck at this stage even longer, because they will be tense as they're practicing, thereby undermining their own learning process. What's worse is if the student begins to believe that the teacher is as frustrated with them as they are with themselves—and as sick of hearing the same appalling noises over and over again. The student may become fearful of their teacher, which also causes them to tense up and produce even more banshee shrieks. But every good teacher knows that this is not a permanent phase for their student; it is merely the awkward beginnings of what could very well go on to be a brilliant violin-playing career. It is just a season, and every season must eventually give way to the next season. Every good teacher remembers that they once produced similar-sounding cacophonies when they first began. And so they have patience for their student. The patience the teacher has for the student should inspire patience in the student for themselves.

The patience of a good teacher is not a passive patience. It's not a sitting-back-and-riding-out-the-storm kind of patience. It's not a patience that hopes that: "this too shall pass—may it be soon!" It is an active, eager patience, a patience that accepts the difficulty of the present, but looks forward to the beauty that is coming; and eagerly desires it. The best teachers will play for their students often, or encourage them to listen to other great violinists—because once the student understands what they could sound like, what they should sound like, they are more fully equipped to eliminate the habits that produce the bad sounds in favor of the ones that produce the glorious sounds.

We have a Teacher who knows first-hand what it is to be a student. And so our Teacher has great patience for us—in fact, He is Patience. Because He Himself was a student, He also knows first-hand that it is possible to get past the squeaks, and reveal the glorious melody that the Father has composed for us to play. He is eager for us to hear the melody (even before we can play it fully) and be constantly inspired by it. His patience is not revealed in Him sitting on the sidelines, quietly waiting for us to get it right. Patience is not the inactive state of waiting for something that may never happen. If we let Him, He will continue to show us how to hold the bow, how to place our fingers, where to apply the correct pressure. His patience is being sure that we will play it one day, and eagerly desiring it; while not negating the full process it will take to get there.

Prompt: In what ways has the Father shown His great patience to you? When we see the Father's patience, our own impatience is revealed. In which places do you need to repent for having been impatient with yourself? Take some time to respond to these questions in your journal.

by ELLA ROSELT / photograph by SYDNEE MELA

YOUR HEART IS A GARDEN

A History Book Prompt by JUSTINA STEVENS

This History Book prompt is for you to practice looking inside your heart with God. When we look with Him, He helps us celebrate growth and understand what's prohibiting it. I love making space for God to see me and help me learn my heart. King David says in the psalms: "You are so intimately aware of me, Lord. You read my heart like an open book and you know all the words I'm about to speak before I even start a sentence! You know every step I will take before my journey even begins. You've gone into my future to prepare the way, and in kindness you follow behind me to spare me from the harm of my past. You have laid your hand on me! This is just too wonderful, deep, and incomprehensible! Your understanding of me brings me wonder and strength" (Psalm 139:3-4, TPT).

Reading this Scripture is so reassuring: God knows us well. Today, we are going to practice trusting this truth. Engaging our faith, our imaginations and our creativity will produce a beautiful outcome.

This prompt is called, "Your Heart is a Garden," and it's pretty simple. Picturing God as a patient Gardener that is tending, repairing and replenishing our gardens is going to be a big part of this prompt. His nearness means He cares, not that He is disappointed. In this prompt, we first must practice welcoming the Gardener in.

1. Go somewhere quiet with your History Book, a pencil and watercolors. Pray this prayer: "God, I welcome you in to help me today. I recognize you do so much in my life when I'm not even aware of it. Today, I breathe in deeply and imagine you as a gardener coming toward me. I practice believing the truth: you are here to love me. I

my history book example

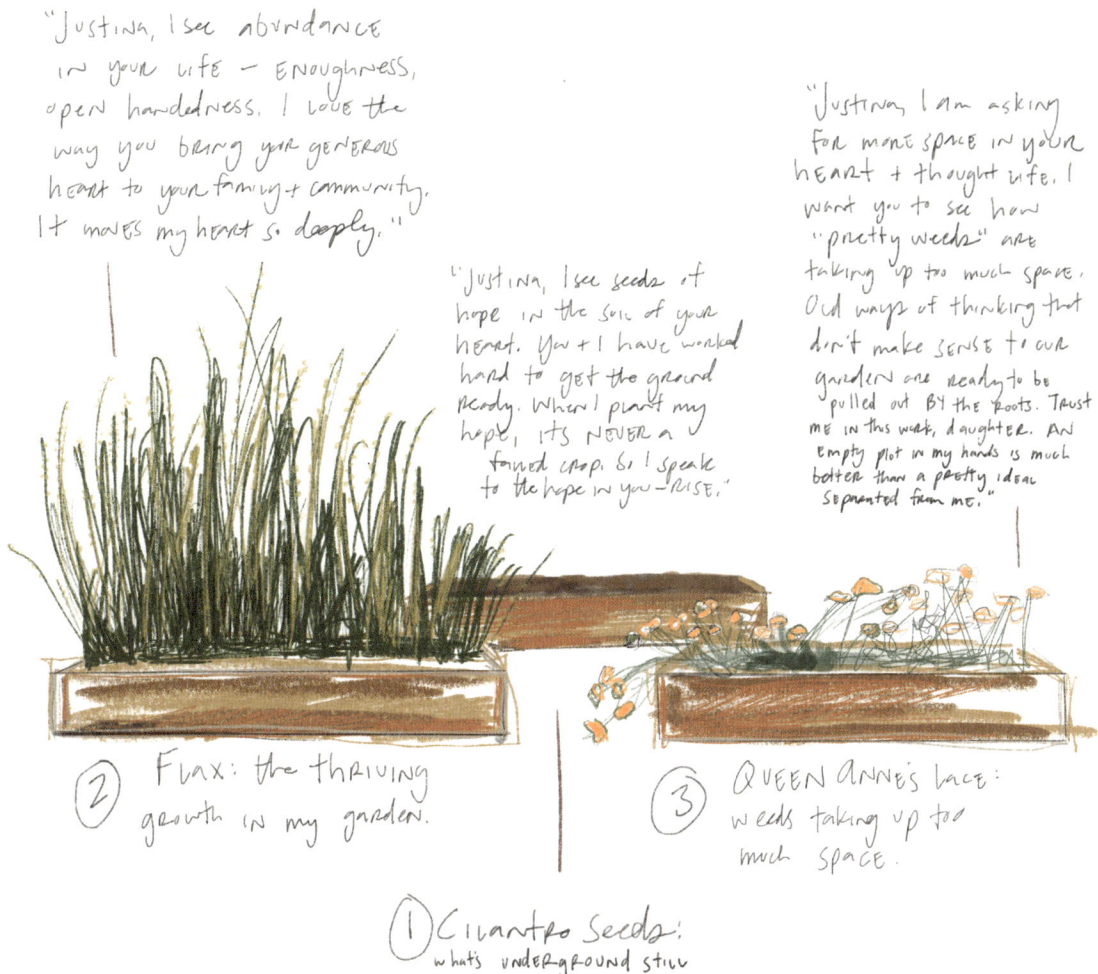

welcome your truth into my life." Ask God these questions and journal His response: "What is still seed under the ground, waiting to emerge? What is thriving in my life? What is taking up too much space in my garden?"

2. Take a deep breath and engage your imagination. Ask God to help you see each of these answers in your garden. Are the seeds in a corner of your garden in well-tilled soil, rocky earth, sand, etc.? What's thriving in your garden, where is it and what kind of plant does it look like? What's taking up too much space, where is it and what kind of plant does it look like? Write out a list like mine: *Seeds:* Cilantro seeds in dark soil—this represents hope. *Thriving:* A big garden box of flax—symbolizing abundance. *Too much space:* Queen Anne's Lace—indicating old ways of thinking.

3. Create three garden boxes that contain the three parts of your garden. Refer to my example. Start your drawing using a pencil and look up images of the plants online. Don't be afraid to try to draw these! This is in your book and it is for you to enjoy. This work is to nourish your relationship with Jesus, not prove your value artistically. Fill your garden boxes with color and label each box.

4. Look over your work and take a deep breath. Pray this prayer: "God, thank you for helping me see the garden of my heart. I submit to you today and ask you to help these seeds grow and be nourished. I ask that you would help me be generous with what is thriving in my garden, I don't want to hoard your blessings. I ask that you would forgive me for letting things overtake space in my garden, I make space for you today. Thank you, Jesus."

FILTERS

by PHYLLIS UNKEFER / photograph by MORGAN CAMPBELL

A RECIPE FOR LISTENING THROUGH NEW FILTERS

I don't often question my ears. With the exception of those nervous hearing tests we took in elementary school that had me agonizing over tiny, barely audible beeps, I haven't generally worried that I wasn't hearing rightly. But more than once, Jesus declared to huge crowds, most of whom had perfectly functioning ears, "Those who have ears to hear, let them hear."

At one point several years ago, He said the same words to me. I was in a tense time, trudging through a lot of pain and discontentment. When I finally stopped to admit that I wasn't finding a way out, I asked a leader in my community for help. I knew she carried wisdom and incisive clarity, and I was grateful when she agreed to start meeting with me. Each week, we sat in her office and she listened while I tried to articulate my tangled thoughts and feelings. The most fruitful thing I did throughout that string of months was to consistently record every meeting. I made voice memos on my phone each time we talked. I only did this for the sake of my memory, but it ended up turning into a revelation for my ears.

Vulnerability has never come easily for me. So to be honest, I was stressed at every one of our meetings. I remember tightly folding my arms and keeping one leg crossed over the other, all tense, as if my body could somehow shield my heart. She had to speak through my walled-off self-protectiveness in order to reach me. But she was patient. And I felt too desperate for help to let stress keep me from pressing in. So each weekend, I listened back to the recording from the previous meeting. And each weekend, I cried.

While listening to our voices, I was coming to the most astonishing awareness: I did not know how to clearly hear. At least not in this instance. There was a distinct difference between what I heard when I sat in her office and what I heard pour through the recording. In person, when she looked me in the eyes and responded honestly to my jungle of thoughts, it seemed to sting. Regardless of what she said, whether it was an observation about my cycling moods or a question to stir a new perspective, I braced myself for her words as if I were under attack. I usually left our meetings feeling a bit scraped up in my soul, for reasons I couldn't quite define. But I cried every time I sat with a recording because it wasn't at all like I'd thought. I heard a wildly different exchange. Her words were kind. Fierce but gentle. There was a profound tenderness in the voice I heard responding to me. She didn't express punishment or judgment; she spoke calmly, with compassion. And as I replayed our conversations, letting them take on an entirely different tone in my memory, I felt Jesus untangling my fears—my apprehensive assumptions that I'd be judged or punished or misunderstood. Through her, He was slowly rinsing those filters from my mind. My defenses came down quietly over time. Every week, I let the true nature of His voice bloom inside my ears. And every week, He was healing how I hear.

For me, that season etched a new depth of self-awareness that I've carried ever since. I'm more aware of my filters. Contrary to what I'd prefer, filters don't usually fall away all at once. So I work on staying conscious of the way I'm hearing in moments of vulnerability, especially with people in positions of authority or leadership. When I start to feel a tightening in my chest and my heart gripping toward defensiveness, I ask myself if I'm perceiving this moment rightly. *Am I hearing this through the lie that leaders are out to attack me?* It tends to shift things considerably when I then reconnect to the truth, *My leaders are for me. They hear me. They aren't against me.* Through truth, I can hear the love in the voices of those around me again. There's a striking connection between my beliefs and my ears. I'm grateful that Jesus is still giving me ears to hear.

Prompt: Go to a quiet space with your journal. Ask God, "What negative filters am I hearing the people I love through? Will you bring up one moment that you want to help me hear in a new way?" Journal His response.

THE VOICE YOU LISTEN TO IS THE ONE THAT DEFINES YOU.

JONATHAN DAVID HELSER

MY EVERYDAY OCEAN

RECIPE FOR RESTORING WONDER
by *JESSIE PHILLIPS* / art by *JUSTINA STEVENS*

Most of my life I grew up near the ocean. Its adventure and wonder were always ten minutes away. I spent weekends and afternoons walking on sand, swimming in the salt and collecting the ocean's gifts. The ocean was a safe place, a favorite place for me. It calmed my soul and brought so much peace. I loved sitting on 39th Avenue on a half-rotted bench, watching the sun kiss the waves goodnight and listening to the songs of the gulls. As I grew older, I continued my routine of visiting my favorite bench, walking the shoreline and soaking in the salty air, but somehow over time it began to lose its magic. I became busier and found myself visiting less and less, the leftover sand in my clothes became an annoyance rather than leftover joy from my day at the beach. My value for this place seemed to become less important as my life became full of more have-to's. The wonder slowly faded away, and taking a day to go to the ocean felt more like a task rather than a gift. I moved away from home when I was eighteen and didn't seem to miss the beach, even though I knew it was something I loved very deeply.

I never gave that transition in my life much thought until a few months ago when it became harder to find the time to go home for visits. I woke up one morning with homesickness in my heart. I imagined myself walking on the familiar shore. The questions started flowing from my heart: *How can it be that ten years later, I'm just realizing the wonder of that place? How am I just recognizing the call to adventure I felt when I was near the ocean? How did I miss it? How did I become blind and numb to the beauty there?* My life is meant to be full of wonder, adventure, excitement and love, and He has set all this up for me to find, even in my routine. My days and heart hold value, even when I don't see it or feel it. That morning was the call to my everyday adventures, realizing the beauty the Lord has set up for me.

The Lord asked me, "Jessie, imagine you have never looked at the ocean before—ever. How would you react? What would you feel? What treasures would you find?" Almost immediately, I was on my knees, crying as I imagined the beauty of the ocean and wrapped my mind around the grandness of that place. I felt the enormity of the water, the splendor of the moment. My heart melted and my eyes were opened again. I was overwhelmed with beauty, adventure, kindness and gratitude. I felt the conviction to never take for granted the routine, no matter how mundane. There are always opportunities waiting for me, gifts waiting to be seen, all put in place by the One who loves adventure more than me. I want to have life and have it more abundantly.

Prompt: What are some routines in your life that have become dull? Invite the Lord to show you how to make them new. What gifts does He have waiting for you there? Ask the Holy Spirit to open your eyes and heart to the beauty in your everyday routine.

THE LANGUAGE OF HANDS

The other morning,
I wanted to talk with You,
To converse
To hear You answer my pressing questions
and with detail instruct my life.
But You were quiet. You only said:

My kindness is here. My gentleness is here.
I'm patient.

I could sense it was not time for so many words.
But in Your silence, I heard a question:
Do you know the language of hands?

Once, I saw a movie where a girl was enraged.
She thrashed with pain, like a flag in a storm.
She was only anchored by her mother's holding
arms, that held and held until she calmed.
Sometimes, the most soothing phrase is curved
inside a palm.

You are teaching me the language of hands
because I'm carried in Yours. You've held and
held through everything.
And at times, my most fluent declaration of
trust is to simply lean.

The other morning I wanted to talk,
but You smiled and showed me Your hands.

Do you know the language of arms that carry
unceasingly?
The crook of Your elbow forms
The warmest of cradles for me.

So yes, I'll let Your kindness wrap around me.
Your gentleness will braid the air.
You'll make a spacious place inside me
by Your hands.

I'm in Your hands.

by PHYLLIS UNKEFER

Cadence, age nine

THE IN BETWEEN

writing and photograph by MELISSA HELSER

Pictures usually inspire my heart to write…pictures I see waiting to happen outside my window, pictures I make with my handy little iPhone or my big Canon Mark II, pictures I create in my mind when beautiful music is playing, pictures I see when looking back through the history of our life—remembering the moments that swept me off my feet and made me remember why I am alive. This morning I was looking back through my photos…and there it was, my Cadence Zion, nine years old, skin golden from the sun, sitting in the waters of the Atlantic Ocean. As a parent, I capture my children with my eyes all the time. Most of these times are when they are not looking. It is the way their hands move or the way they smile when no one is around and they amuse themselves, or maybe when they look at you and all at once you feel love like you've never felt before. I feel like a constant camera, always asking the Holy Spirit to help me savor this life I have with them. I ask that He would keep me alert and alive, that my eyes could be kissed with eternity. "…He has planted eternity in the human heart…" (Ecclesiastes 3:11, NLT). How do we connect with eternity in everyday life? I am on a journey to feel eternity here on this earth, in the real soil of life. Cadence Zion here in this moment…I caught him in the in-between. In-between what? I can't remember. It doesn't matter. Oh that every season would be my favorite. That I would look back on life and feel overwhelmed by the goodness of God to invite me into motherhood. Life is moving, always. May we get into the flow of the beauty of it—that we would trade in our heaviness for a weightless grace to love deep.

The Power of Scripture

by JESSIE MILLER
art by MORGAN CAMPBELL

"All Scripture is inspired by God and is useful to teach us what is true and to make us realize what is wrong in our lives. It corrects us when we are wrong and teaches us to do what is right. God uses it to prepare and equip his people to do every good work" (II Timothy 3:16-17, NLT).

We've all done it. "God, please speak to me as I randomly open my Bible. Please let this page have the answer I'm looking for." Hopefully, you just made a knowing smile. It's so easy to do! The Bible is full of wisdom and answers to help us in our time of need, but so often, we disconnect from its Author and treat it like a Magic 8 Ball. We want to hear what we want to hear, when we want to hear it. And we will "shake it" again and again if we don't like the answer we get.

This kind of approach to the Bible has led many to blatantly or subtly regard it as unnecessary, disappointing or incapable of holding timeless truth. When we treat it as something to be manipulated, we give it very little power to help transform our lives. Scripture was not meant to be weaponized for our own agendas. It was not meant to pull us from intimacy with God—*I don't need to ask God about His Word, I just read it.* I have found in my own life that the Lord's voice comes alive in the complementary practices of listening to His words to me personally through journaling His voice and meditating on His words and way given to us in Scripture. I need His voice that specifically speaks to the things that are on my heart. I need the perspective and promises from His Word to hold fast to, that have stood the test of time and transcend my current maturity. God so deeply wants to reach us, to help us, to guide us, to comfort us and reveal truth. So, where do we start? How do we begin to let God's Word really affect us? Here are some keys that have served me as I've read the Word of God:

First, approach it with wonder and reverence. Scripture is a direct reflection of the brilliance of our God. He knows we need Him and He knows that we need each other. He has woven truth into the written Word so that for centuries we could learn from and through one another about Him—the Alpha and Omega, the Beginning and End. Our relational God wants you to feel the miracle of the story you are a part of. We serve a God who did not leave us in the dark, but offers us guidance and peace, clarity and correction, love and affirmation. As you unfold your Bible in your lap, or open it on your phone, remember, you're holding a miracle—a sign and a wonder that the God of the universe wants to make His words come alive and take root in you. Start with a deep breath of gratitude and a prayer, "Lord, I want to be affected."

Secondly, expect that it will invite you to change. Yes, God accepts us as we are, but He did not create us as stagnant beings. He created us to grow, to transform through the power of the Holy Spirit and the sacrifice of Jesus into something greater, into a truer version of ourselves. Therefore, when we read, we want to take time to ask God, "What are you saying to me through this Scripture? How does this affect me today?" According to Paul, you can expect to experience "teaching, rebuking, correcting and training in righteousness, so that the servant of God may be thoroughly equipped for every good work" (II Timothy 3:16-17, NIV). Scripture is meant to spark dialogue with God and others. Be open to the action God will offer your heart and trust the grace He will provide to move forward. "Don't just listen to the Word of Truth and not respond to it, for that is the essence of self-deception. So always let his Word become like poetry written and fulfilled by your life!" (James 1:22, TPT)

Thirdly, seek to take it to memory. "I have hidden your word in my heart that I might not sin against you" (Psalm 119:11, NIV). Ask the Lord to lead you to specific verses or passages that speak to what He is teaching you right now. Memorize them and dwell on them through the day as you fight the lies of the enemy and practice believing new truth. Jesus in His time on earth, even while having complete access to God and His thoughts, chose to cherish and dwell on Scripture. He let it direct, encourage and fill Him. He used it to fight the enemy and to bring clarity as He taught and ministered. Even from the Cross, He clung to David's words from Psalm 22. We know the beginning, "My God, my God, why have you forsaken me?" But He knew the rest of the psalm and clung to it. He let Himself follow the depths of David's pain as He went through His own, and then let Himself rise with the same hope and trust in the Lord and ended by declaring the last line of the psalm, "He has done it!" or, "It is finished." Friends, if Jesus let Scripture anchor His heart, how much more should we?

And finally, enjoy it! God's Word is a way He can always reach us and offer us a place to start in our relationship with Him. He wants us to know that we originated in His design. He wants us to see how He has fought for relationship with us from the very beginning. He wants us to be able to marvel at how He unfolded our story of redemption generation after generation and let it fill us with courage that He is faithful and worthy to be trusted. He wants to help us. He wants to see us thriving. This should fill our hearts with joy and hope as we read. God has been thinking about us since the beginning and wants to encounter us daily as we invite Him to speak, and learn to take pleasure in His company.

Prompt: Ask God for one Scripture that you can practice these four keys with. I love asking God for a Scripture to anchor my seasons. Commit to returning to this same Scripture every day for an entire week. Practice approaching it with reverence, expecting it will invite you to change, memorizing it and enjoying it.

EYES TO SEE

RECIPE FOR NEW PERSPECTIVE
writing and photography by CHRIS MILLER

As a young boy, I would eagerly look forward to extended visits with my grandparents. Time spent at their home was precious to me and it meant Grandma's homemade cookies, ice cold Kool-Aid and tagging along outside with my grandfather as he worked. I slept in a guest room that opened up into the living room and would often wake up to the sound of the television reporters mumbling the early morning news through the hollow wooden door. I would tumble out of bed and into their living room to find my grandfather patiently untangling a 1,000+ piece puzzle. Standing at his side, I'd watch with amazement as he revealed lush landscapes and beautiful mountainous scenes out of hundreds of tiny, colored cardboard shapes. Excited, I'd ask to help, and would fumble through the jigsaw pieces, my tiny fingers attempting to construct corners of the picture with the few shapes that I could make out. It sometimes felt impossible, and I'd be frustrated when I couldn't decode the image on my own. Piece by piece, my patient grandfather would help me create a beautiful picture out of a mess of colors and shapes.

What has taken me years to understand is that my grandfather was teaching me how to see. He would study the master image on the box until he knew it and it was in his heart. When he put his hand to the pieces, he had vision and a clear direction. He knew where he was going and he wasn't in a hurry. In those early morning hours, he taught me to do the same.

How often do we stumble into our days, grasping at the fugitive pieces of our lives, flustered by the size and scope? We have hopes, fears, dreams, glimpses, ideas and thoughts, but don't know where we are going. We feel like a mess of pieces scattered across the surface of life.

I believe that every day is a new invitation to come to the Father with childlike faith and trust Him with all of the pieces of our lives.

I believe that every day is a new invitation to come to the Father with childlike faith and trust Him with all of the pieces of our lives. I have come to see the Father as the patient de-puzzler of my mind and heart. The enemy is constantly bombarding me with fragmented and anxious ways of seeing the world and myself. He'd like me to believe that I am alone and that the mess of me is too much to untangle. All the while I have a faithful Father who is patient and full of love. I have a Father who sees me, loves me and knows me.

Prompt: Do you feel like your life is a scattered mess of pieces? What do you believe God sees when He looks at you?

I believe that God wants to bring clarity, confirm truth and restore your vision. Give Him the pieces and watch as He patiently creates something beautiful out of your life. Find a quiet place and ask the Father what He sees when He looks at you. What are His thoughts about you?

Begin to write down what you hear Him speaking into your heart. Let courage fill you as the patient hand of God teaches you how to see.

Shorts *to inspire* five *minute* moments

SEE AGAIN
by EMILY PELL

I love to go on walks with God. The quiet and the steady pace help me clear my mind and listen to my heart. Recently, while walking in the woods, I passed a cedar stump and felt a holy pause come over me. I took a moment to look at the stump again and let the color impact me. God spent so much time creating the layers of reds and purples in the grain. It moved me. I felt like I got to stop and *be* with God, appreciating something He spent time making.

Today, go on a walk or find an ordinary spot—somewhere you pass by every day—and ask the Holy Spirit to show you something brand new that you may have missed before. Then, thank Him for eyes to see again.

TOOLS & TEACHERS
by LUKE SKAGGS

Tools are meant to help us, not to be an indicator of stupidity. Asking for help from a good teacher is one of the wisest things we can do. Help saves us time and keeps us safe. We have been given the best Teacher, the Holy Spirit!

"If the Lord had not been my helper, I would have quickly become silent" (Psalm 94:17, ISV).

Sit with Him, the Master Craftsman, and ask Him where the places are in your life that you've tried to figure things out on your own. Repent and then invite Him into those spaces to be your Teacher. Ask for His help. Journal His voice over you as a gentle Teacher.

WINTER TREE
by KATELAND CASE

When a tree has lost all its leaves and bares itself, you see its true form. This tree is stepping into winter, yet it stands tall and firm for what is about to come. It knows that the summer brought great beauty with green foliage; and the fall brought great calming joy with its autumn colors bursting forth. Yet in winter, the tree will carry nothing to cover its branches. Its entire form will be exposed. It may seem scary, but the tree knows it needs the winter because it brings growth inside the trunk and roots. In the winter, no one can see the great growth that happens.

Take a moment and ask the Father what He is growing in you in this season that no one else can see but you and Him. Let it be a reminder for whatever season that He knows all things happening within; and throughout it all, He is your consistent Friend.

POPPY
by ALLIE SAMPSON

For many years, I've admired the simple beauty of a flower called Anemone coronaria. Chances are you've noticed it, too. They carry bold color without any pretense. This captivating flower is more commonly known as the poppy.

I believe names are significant. I appreciate that science has gifted us with formal names for living things in addition to the more common name by which we know them. Do you know what your name means? Take some time to research or revisit the meaning of your name. Then ask the Father what He knows you by. What does He call you? Journal His voice and relish in the truth that you are named and known by God.

art by JUSTINA STEVENS

SONG OF THE MORNING

by LINDSAY VANCE

Between the kiss of Earth and Sun
Falls the sound of freedom

Dust awaken
Light behold
The new song of morning

Inside unspoken words of God
Man finds his redemption

Sunken eyes
Black with sleep
Earth is lost in waters deep
'Til clear vision set beneath
Emerges from the song of morning

Beating drum
Chord and string
Father's footstep, mother's wing
My heart alights and I sing
I live the song of morning

CROPS

A RECIPE FOR PARTNERING WITH THE LORD

What a joy it is to drive a rural road lined with farms and fields as far as the eye can see. Growing up in the farmlands of North Carolina, this became one of my very favorite things to do. It was normal to daily pass wide open fields planted with anything from cotton or soybeans to peanuts or sweet potatoes. Long rows in wide, sandy soil, filled with the sprouting, growing seed of whatever crop the farmer had sown.

Are not our hearts just like these farm fields? A deep space of rich dirt, ready in each season for whatever the Father is sowing and cultivating in our lives. He prepares the soil, adding nutrients, disking and tilling, readying our hearts for the cultivation and the stretching that every new season brings. Seasons come and go and the faithful Farmer is committed to see your heart flourish.

Prompt: Sit with the Lord and ask Him what He is cultivating in your heart in this season of your life. Is He growing a familiar crop, wooing you to grow in more maturity? Has He planted seed that will lead to new revelation? Is He opening your eyes to see Him in new ways? Ask the Father how you can partner with Him, cultivating growth in your heart and caring for the seed that He has planted.

by MARTHA MCRAE

> "THE RAIN CAME DOWN, THE STREAMS ROSE, AND THE WINDS BLEW AND BEAT AGAINST THAT HOUSE; YET IT DID NOT FALL, BECAUSE IT HAD ITS FOUNDATION ON THE ROCK."
>
> MATTHEW 7:25, NIV

"WE ESCAPED LIKE A BIRD FROM A HUNTER'S TRAP. THE TRAP IS BROKEN, AND WE ARE FREE!" PSALM 124:7

ABOUT

The Cageless Birds is a missional community of leaders and artisans from Sophia, North Carolina founded by Jonathan and Melissa Helser. We are drawn together by an authentic passion for the Gospel of Jesus and a commitment to live out wholeness in community. We believe in the risk of saying yes to flying out of the cage of fear and soaring on the wings of true identity. We are committed to pouring our lives out in ministry for the sake of the Gospel and dedicated to the continued process of spiritual formation.

Our discipleship school, the 18 Inch Journey, exists to see sons and daughters liberated by the love of God. Our schools, retreats and camps exist to close the gap between what we know about God in our heads and who we believe Him to be in our hearts. Here, we set a table for people from all over the world to encounter the Father, practice honesty and vulnerability with Jesus, learn the emotional health tools that have changed our lives and experience the transformation that happens in community.

As artisans, we come alive in creating goods throughout the year that help support the mission of our schools. Whether it's recording music, writing books or cultivating one of our many other art forms, we are anchored with joy in the pursuit of excellence in all that we do. For more on the Cageless Birds, visit our website and online store at cagelessbirds.com.

2022 CONTRIBUTORS

JONATHAN DAVID HELSER
MELISSA HELSER
JUSTINA STEVENS
JAKE STEVENS
JD GRAVITT
ERIN GRAVITT
JESSIE PHILLIPS
CHRIS MILLER
JESSIE MILLER
JOEL CASE
KATELAND CASE
MOLLY SKAGGS
ELLA ROSELT
LINDSAY VANCE
ALLIE SAMPSON
PHYLLIS UNKEFER
MARY HALL
MARTHA MCRAE
SYDNEE MELA
LUKE SKAGGS
MORGAN CAMPBELL
EMILY PELL
KEN HELSER
CADENCE HELSER
GRAHAM COOKE
GABRIEL RAMIREZ

CREDITS

EDITOR-IN-CHIEF
Melissa Helser

ART DIRECTION AND GRAPHIC DESIGN
Melissa Helser, Justina Stevens & Morgan Campbell

COPY EDITORS
Allie Sampson, Phyllis Unkefer
Hannah MacSorley, Mary Hall,
Justina Stevens & Jessie Miller

PHOTO EDITOR
Morgan Campbell

COVER ART
Justina Stevens

HANDLETTERED TYPE
Justina Stevens

TABLE OF CONTENTS ART
Justina Stevens & Morgan Campbell

BIBLIOGRAPHY

1-2 Cultivate definition: "cultivate." Merriam-Webster.com. Merriam-Webster, 2016.
3 Allender, Dan B., and Tremper Longman. The Cry of the Soul: How Our Emotions Reveal Our Deepest Questions about God. NavPress, 2015.
4 Augustine, of Hippo, Saint, 354-430. The Confessions of Saint Augustine.
5 Dodd, Chip. The Voice of the Heart: A Call to Full Living. Sage Hill, LLC, 2014.
6 Relief definition: "relief." Merriam-Webster.com. Merriam-Webster, 2022.
7 Manning, Brennan. The Furious Longing of God. David C. Cook, 2009.
8 Savor definition: "savor." Google.com. Google, 2014.

About Page Scripture: Psalm 124:7, NLT.

All rights reserved.
No portion of this book may be reproduced without permission from the Cageless Birds.
Published in 2013. Revised 2022.

THE COLLECTION

Discover all the volumes of Cultivate at cagelessbirds.com.

I. THE HEAD TO HEART JOURNEY

The revised Head to Heart Journey, Volume I, is an introduction to journaling the voice of the Lord, settling into true identity and exploring the terrain of your heart with God. Volume I unpacks the foundational values we build on in our other Cultivate devotionals.

II. THE CLARITY WINTER BRINGS

Designed to help you find beauty in quieter seasons of the heart, this book includes writings on topics such as hope, patience, perspective and stillness and is meant to encourage you to hear His voice in the midst of bare seasons.

III. FLY HIGH. BUILD HOME.

Created to bring understanding to what it means to live a sustainable life, this volume will explore what it means to thrive—to soar in the seemingly mundane moments of your life as well as the big-picture occasions.

IV. CREATIVITY UNLOCKED

Words and prompts that empower you to take risks in expression and discover your creative ability. These writings are meant to challenge your idea of what creativity is and unlock the truth that creativity is a birthright, not a skill-set.

V. THE ART OF CONNECTION, PT. I

Written with your most significant relationships in mind, Volume V is designed to encourage and empower you to pursue healthy and thriving relationships in dating, marriage, parenting and relating to your parents. May these writings inspire you with courage, hope and healthy perspective for God-centered relationships with those who mean the most to you.

VI. THE ART OF CONNECTION, PT. II

Centered around core themes of self-awareness, communication and generosity, Volume VI is designed to inspire transformative conversations with the Lord and propel you toward powerful, healthy relationships in every area of your life. It offers practical tools for how to maintain healthy connection with close friends, team, co-workers, acquaintances and strangers.

CONNECT + SUPPORT

TO PURCHASE COPIES
and other Cageless Birds goods
go to cagelessbirds.com or amazon.com

INSTAGRAM
@cagelessbirds

**DISCIPLESHIP RETREATS
AND SCHOOLS**
18inchjourney.com

WHOLESALE AND QUESTIONS
store@cagelessbirds.com